THE WHY? COURSE

A THREE-PART INTRODUCTION TO CHRISTIANITY

Fr Marcus Holden
MA (Oxon), STL
Archdiocese of Southwark
Director of the MA in Apologetics, Maryvale

Fr Andrew Pinsent
MA (Oxon), DPhil, STB, PhL, PhD
Diocese of Arundel and Brighton
Theology and Religion Faculty, Oxford University

Catholic Truth Society

Acknowledgements The authors from the Evangelium Project extend their thanks to the Catholic Truth Society, especially the members of the editorial board and staff who encouraged the development of the WHY? course. Special thanks are due to Fergal Martin, Pierpaolo Finaldi, Richard Brown, Simone Finaldi, Stephen Campbell, Llima Cole, Christine Parreno and Glenda Sincock. They also wish to express their gratitude to St Anthony Communications and especially to Christian and Emily Holden and Nick Curtis. They also thank all those who have contributed to the WHY? Course in a variety of ways: Catherine Anderson, Michael d'Arcy, Martin Arumemi-Ikhide, Fr Richard Biggerstaff, Jamie Bogle, Joanna Bogle, Marie Burbidge, Jenna Cooper, Sr Hyacinthe Defos du Rau, Kieron Driver, Bruno Ebe, Jordan Evans, Anne Howard, William Johnstone, John Kimber, Jerry Naunheim, James Newcombe, William Newton, Mary Nolan, Stephanie Pena, Hellena Taylor, Fr Ed Tomlinson, Hannah Vaughan-Spruce, Peter Williams and Ian Wordley. The authors are grateful to their bishops, the Rt Rev. Kieran Conry and Most Rev. Peter Smith, and to the many priests and deacons who have encouraged, promoted and co-operated on this project in many ways. Above all, the authors thank their parents, John and Irene Holden, and Charles and Teresa Pinsent, for their constant support, prayer and guidance.

CTS books explain the faith, teaching and life of the Catholic Church. They are based on Sacred Scripture, the Second Vatican Council documents, and the *Catechism of the Catholic Church*. Our books provide authentic Catholic teaching; they address issues of life and of truth which are relevant to all. They aim to inform and educate readers on the many issues that people have to deal with today.

In addition, CTS nurtures and supports the Christian life through its many spiritual, liturgical, educational and pastoral books. As Publisher to the Holy See, CTS publishes the official documents of the Catholic Church as they are issued.

Dedication: The WHY? course is dedicated to Fr John Redford of the Maryvale Institute, a great catechist and apologist, who has devoted many decades of his life and work to communicating the riches of the Catholic faith.

References to the *Catechism of the Catholic Church*, the official catechism promulgated by Pope John Paul II, are marked "ccc." followed by the number of the paragraph. References to the *Compendium of the Catechism* are marked "*Compendium*". Besides standard printed and bound versions, the English text of the catechism and its compendium are available at the time of publication on the official Vatican website. Scripture references are taken from the *Revised Standard Version Catholic Edition*, with occasional and slight modifications of certain New Testament passages made directly from the Greek text, in line with other standard translations. The key books cited and their abbreviations are: Genesis (*Gn*); Exodus (*Ex*); Numbers (*Nb*); Deuteronomy (*Dt*); 1-2 Samuel (*1-2 S*); 1-2 Kings (*1-2 K*); Psalms (*Ps*); Isaiah (*Is*); Matthew (*Mt*); Mark (*Mk*); Luke (*Lk*); John (*Jn*); Acts of the Apostles (*Ac*); Romans (*Rm*); 1 Corinthians (*1 Co*); 2 Corinthians (*2 Co*); Galatians (*Ga*); Ephesians (*Ep*); Philippians (*Ph*); Colossians (*Col*); Thessalonians (*1 Th*); 2 Thessalonians (*2 Th*); 1 Timothy (*1 Tm*); 2 Timothy (*2 Tm*); Letter to the Hebrews (*Heb*); James (*Jm*); 1 Peter (*1 P*); 2 Peter (*2 P*); 1 John (*1 Jn*); Book of Revelation (*Rv*).

ISBN: 978 1 86082 883 6

CTS Code: EV7

To accompany THE WHY? COURSE Book:

THE WHY? COURSE DVD

EAN: 5060139000123

CTS Code: EV8

Contents

OPENING PRAYER

As the final goal of Christian teaching is to know God, it is good to ask for God's help at the beginning of each session of the WHY? course. The following short prayer is from St Thomas Aquinas, who always prayed before study.

**Bestow upon me, O God,
an understanding that knows you,
wisdom in finding you, a way of life that is pleasing to you,
perseverance that faithfully waits for you,
and confidence that I shall embrace you at the last.**

Amen.

Part I: Watch

Watch one of the three films of the WHY? course, each one of which lasts no more than 25 minutes. If you are using the course in a group, a presenter may briefly introduce the session.

Part II: Reflect

Reflect on the film, which may be done in various ways, for example: (1) re-read one or more parts of the transcript (pages 7-47), including the background material on the facing pages; (2) read the example questions alongside the transcript, ask yourself if the challenges are good ones and how you think a Catholic might respond, and finally check the model answers at the back of this course book (pages 48-60); (3) think about the meaning of key words highlighted in the transcript and check your conclusions against the glossary at the back of the course book (pages 61-64). If you are using the course in a group, it will often be helpful to share your observations with other participants and to ask your own questions to encourage discussion of the issues raised. At the end of the session, the presenter may offer a brief summary and prayer.

Introduction

God, Christ and the Catholic Church he founded are arguably the most fascinating subjects that one can study, shaping the development of civilisation, culture, ideas, language, ethics and even the very concepts of history and time. Moreover, from the perspective of the faith, Christ and his Church offer the priceless gift of eternal salvation with God and the saints in heaven. Many people in the world today, however, have never had the opportunity for informed enquiry into these matters and face the challenges of work and other pressures that allow them little time for study.

The WHY? course has been written to provide this opportunity by presenting an introduction to the Catholic Faith in three easy sessions by means of a DVD and course book. The course is designed for a wide range of users, in groups or as individuals, and no special training is required. Each of the three sessions, "Why God? Why Christ? Why the Church?" has two parts: **Watch** and **Reflect** (see opposite).

What does this WHY? course book provide?

The main sections of this course book (pages 7-47), a copy of which is intended for each participant in the WHY? course, provide you with:

- A transcript of the main interviews of the films on the DVD, enabling you to read and think about what the speakers are saying at your own pace.

- Additional background and reference material on the facing pages, offering you the opportunity to explore the issues raised in more detail.

- Accompanying questions to challenge some of the claims made by speakers, to encourage your reflections and possible group discussions.

- A cross-referenced set of model answers to these questions (pages 48-60), offering you typical Catholic responses to these challenges.

- A glossary with a brief explanation of key Catholic religious words used by speakers (pages 61-64), to assist with understanding the interviews.

In the three main sections of the course book, some KEY WORDS in the transcripts of the interviews are also highlighted in capitals and explained in the glossary.

We hope you will enjoy this opportunity and that you will find your exploration of the faith to be fruitful. After completing the WHY? course, the final page of this book offers some suggestions as to what can be done next. A copy of a Catholic Bible and also the *Catechism of the Catholic Church* may be helpful for reading and as reference texts if you want to study further. Moreover, there is also a wealth of other resources available from the Evangelium Project, including the *Credo* pocket catechism and the full *Evangelium* course itself. Above all, we hope that your exploration of the faith will help lead you to eternal life, *"These things are written that you may believe that Jesus is the Christ, the Son of God, and that believing you may have life in his name"* (Jn 20:31).

Why is there something rather than nothing?
Why is there order rather than disorder?

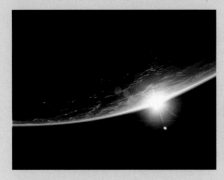

Sunrise from space: the movements of planets and stars can be described by precise mathematical laws.

Living things develop in a kind of creative tension, with harmony emerging from spontaneity and change.

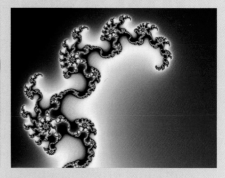

The invisible and formal world of mathematics has its own beauty revealed by modern computers.

The search for 'because' (the 'cause-of-being') and for a first or ultimate cause of all things

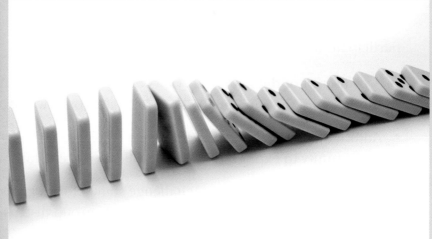

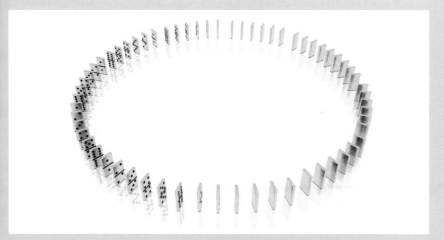

There is nothing that we know of in the universe that is self-causing. All things are caused by other things, like a domino that has to be pushed by another domino in order to topple over (top-right). But this chain of causes cannot continue forever, or there would be no beginning, middle or end. Nor can all the causes operating in the universe go in a circle (bottom-right), because the circle as a whole does not cause itself either. So philosophers like Aristotle (left) came to the conclusion that there must be a 'first cause', something that causes everything else without itself being caused - and this is what human beings naturally call 'God'.

Why God?

Does God exist?

By nature we desire to know not just what things are but why they are. People ask such questions of the things around us, but many have dared to ask, "Why is there something rather than nothing? Why am I here at all? Where am I going?" These are big questions which need big answers.

1. Why should I care if God exists or not?

Today many people struggle with atheism and agnosticism but remain unsatisfied. The search for **GOD** and the enquiry into whether God is real is not something that people only did in times past but is relevant to people throughout time and throughout the world.

We can know that God exists through reason, not just through **FAITH**, as is clear from the world around us. We see so many things that change, that come and go. They don't have to be there. They might not be there in the future. But for anything to be there at all, for there to be something rather than nothing, there has to be one thing, one principle that must be - that has to be. This principle cannot be material, because all material things by their nature come and go. It must be a **SPIRITUAL** principle - which we call God.

2. Surely the universe just *is*? We don't need to know anything else to explain it.

Some people talk today as if the existence of God is a new or serious problem, but in fact most philosophers throughout most of human history have held that there is a God, and that we can prove there is a God.

3. Surely intelligent people today don't believe in God?

Most of the Western intellectual tradition started with two ancient Greek philosophers, Plato and Aristotle. They helped to shape many of our institutions. They invented biology, they helped to invent logic, and we still draw from a lot of their thoughts today. Both Plato and Aristotle, in different ways, hold that there is a God. For Plato, God was the 'Form of the Good'. For Aristotle, the other great founder of the Western intellectual tradition, God is that which moves everything else but is not himself moved. He puts everything else into motion and causes the changes that we see in the world. Aristotle said that God is good, and God is perfect, and God is eternal.

For the **Answers to Questions** turn to page 48.

Why do we need God when we have the Big Bang theory, genetics and evolution to explain existence?

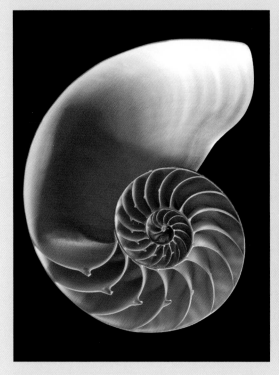 

All scientific theories, including the Big Bang theory, genetics and evolution, describe how some physical things are transformed into other physical things, but not why any things exist in the first place. So there is still a need for a 'first cause' or 'God'. The order of the cosmos also strongly suggests intelligent creative action, even though God may bring about this order partly through natural processes with their own spontaneity. Moreover, Catholics have contributed in important ways to understanding these processes. For example, the Big Bang theory and genetics were first proposed by the Catholic priests Georges Lemaître and Gregor Mendel, respectively. In addition, one of the first persons to suggest that God's creation 'evolves' (from a Latin word *evolvere* meaning 'to unfold') was St Augustine, Bishop of Hippo in North Africa in the early fifth century.

Fr Georges Lemaître with Albert Einstein, 1933.
Fr Lemaître applied Einstein's equations of relativity to propose what is now known as the Big Bang theory of the origin of the universe.

Fr Gregor Mendel, the 'Father of Genetics', c.1880.
Fr Mendel's meticulous observations of the inherited characteristics of plants laid the foundations of modern genetics.

We can know that there is a God from what we can see in the universe, from the way in which everything that is necessary for life holds together so perfectly - oxygen, water and so on. Everything holds together, not in a ghastly tension, but in a rich creative tension that enables things to grow and evolve. Everything that is in the universe is perfectly ordered, and man can know this order. Our own minds tell us that there is a great intellect at work here, and as man explores, as we do now, the stars and solar system, we discover more and more about the perfection of the cosmos. This work speaks to us of God, of the great creative mind.

4. Isn't the universe full of chaos, disorder and blind chance?

Einstein once said that God was the cause of the intelligibility of the universe - an elaborate way of saying that the universe is filled with meaning and purpose, and we are amazing because we can discern this purposeful action. In the **BIBLE** it is said that God made the world: the word that is used is *poema* (*Ep* 2:10), from which we get the word 'poem'. It is from the poetry of the world that we understand the poet and from the artistry that we understand the artist. Many people come to a belief in God just through seeing this artistry in things.

5. If the universe is filled with purpose, why can't we see what this purpose is?

One of the most popular proofs of the existence of God is the so-called 'Cosmological Proof', which works as follows. Nothing that we see and we know of in the universe causes itself. All these things are caused by something else, and you can play a game with this principle. Look at the things around us: none of them cause themselves, they are all caused by something else. As you work backwards, you ask, "What caused the things that caused those things, and what caused the things that caused the things that caused those things?" You work backwards and backwards but eventually you have to come to a stopping point, some first cause that causes everything else, without itself being caused. What is interesting is that this inference that the universe has a first cause is very much part of Catholic philosophy. This inference may also have helped to influence our belief in the Big Bang, because the Big Bang theory was developed by a Catholic priest, Fr Georges Lemaître. This development was not popular among atheists and many of them rejected the Big Bang theory for thirty or forty years. For the Catholic priest who had proposed the theory, however, it was perfectly reasonable that the universe could have a beginning, a cause, and that the cosmos wasn't always the way it is today.

6. If God causes everything, what caused God?

For the **Answers to Questions** turn to pages 48-49.

What is the problem of evil and suffering?

The Penitent Magdalene by Georges de La Tour (left) and *Job Rebuked by His Friends* by William Blake (right)

The figure of Mary Magdalene on the left illustrates the problem of death, symbolised by the skull, and the moral evil of sin or wrongdoing, suggested by the turning away of the face from the viewer in shame, and the mirror, a symbol of vanity. The solitary, burning candle can be interpreted as a symbol of hope, but may also warn of the ebbing away of time until the light of life is extinguished and darkness descends. The image of Job on the right illustrates the moral challenge of the perfect man who is reduced to wretched misery, proclaiming his innocence while rebuked by his friends.

Although the study of physics, mathematics and cosmology may inspire wonder and even religious awe, the study of living things, including ourselves, raises some difficult questions. If there is a good and all-powerful God, why is there so much waste, suffering, disease and death? The problem is not just that good creatures go wrong but that so many creatures seem predetermined to cause suffering and death to other creatures. Moreover, human beings also appear predetermined to evil, not just in suffering but in inflicting harm. For instance, the same human race that has composed heart-wrenchingly beautiful music has also inflicted pointless cruelty, torture and death on millions of fellow human beings in concentration camps. Although some suffering may be praiseworthy, such as that of the athlete in training, and some may be grimly necessary, such as the punishments of heinous criminals, much appears to be endured against their will by those who are innocent. Why does God not intervene?

The Lord Answering Job out of the Whirlwind by William Blake

One way to address this question is to see what God has to say about this problem in the revealed books of those who believe in him. Perhaps the most famous such account is the Book of Job, the biblical story of a perfectly innocent man crushed by suffering. When God answers Job's complaints at the end of the book (*Jb* 38-41), he does so mainly by rhetorical questions about the grandeur of creation, *"Where were you when I laid the foundation of the earth?"* (38:4). This larger perspective, the transformation of Job's relationship to God and the fact he obtains new blessings at the end of the book, hints at the beginning of one response to the problem of evil: we have to see the larger picture and the end of the story.

Many of the greatest minds in history believed in God. Aristotle thought of God as the first mover, Plato as the unchangeable good, and Isaac Newton as the architect of the laws of the universe. Louis Pasteur, the inventor of pasteurisation, once said that a little science estranges men from God, but much science brings them back to him.

One of the best ways to discover God is looking at the creature we know best: the human creature. We discover something more in human beings than we find in any other creature in the world, either animate or inanimate. We realise, for example, that we have freedom, intellect and love. These are spiritual capacities of the **SOUL** that point to God in a very direct way. We can realise that we're made like God. God can't be anything less than these qualities. He must have them in order to give them.

7. Hasn't modern science shown that human beings are simply clever animals?

Why is there evil in the world?

For most people, it is not enough to state positive reasons why there must be a God. They ask the much more personal question, "What difference does this God make?" They may struggle with feelings of distance and alienation from God, and, when they see so much suffering and **EVIL**, they may doubt that there is a good and loving God.

8. What if I don't want to be with God, or don't feel any alienation at all?

For most of us, the question of suffering is at the core of our questions about God and about religious faith. If there is a God, and if this God is good, how can he permit suffering? This question relates to our deepest experiences in our own lives, those of the people near to us, and to human history, which seems to be one long saga of suffering.

As soon as we resolve one problem - we invent antibiotics or anaesthetics - we seem to come up with another one like nuclear war. We manage to eliminate torture in one country, only for it to appear in another. What is in us that warps our behaviour? We understand that there is something in human beings that is not quite right. We are not at peace with ourselves, and nature is not at peace in the way that it should be either, with volcanic eruptions and so on. So this question of suffering is the deepest one; it relates to, "Is there a deity and, if so, of what nature is this God and does he care about us? How do we fit into God's plans?"

9. There may be a lack of peace in the world, but how can God be the answer when religions are so different from one another and bring so much division?

For the **Answers to Questions** turn to page 49.

What else does religion say about evil and suffering?

The Garden of Eden by Jacob de Backer

The Fall of the Rebel Angels by Pieter Bruegel the Elder

Genesis, the first book of the Bible, begins with a revealed symbolic history in which the world is initially created good. When human beings chose freely to break God's only command to them, eating the forbidden fruit, they also rejected God's love, losing paradise and beginning a life of suffering, ignorance and discontent, ending in death (*Gn* 3). The last book of the Bible, Revelation, claims that some of the powerful, contingent spiritual beings that God has created, called 'angels', have also rebelled and are ultimately responsible for an on-going war against God on earth (*Rv* 12). From these narratives, at least two initial responses to the problem of evil and suffering emerge. First, that God is the first but not the only cause of all things that happen in the world, since intellectual beings have been given the dignity of free will. Second, the abuse of this freedom has evil consequences by means of the causes and effects that God has implanted in the world. Genesis does hint early on that God will offer a means of salvation for humanity (*Gn* 3:15), but there is no return to Eden (*Gn* 3:24).

The Garden of Earthly Delights by Hieronymus Bosch

The painting above illustrates symbolically the degeneration of humanity separated from God. Created initially in a state of innocence and natural perfection (left), human beings lose friendship with God as a result of sin. At first, they continue to use their freedom and delight in the things that God has created (centre). Nevertheless, already there are signs of perversion and futility in this carnival of activity, which culminates in chaos and the tortures of damnation (right). This sequence suggests another response to the problem of at least some suffering: a God who loves us might well make use of suffering to suspend the carnival of delights, disturbing us in order to rescue us from a descent into destruction.

Had God wanted to, he could have given us no choice in life. He could have programmed us only to do good, but then we would only have been robots, acting only by the will of another. Instead he gave us **FREE WILL**, the capacity to choose for ourselves, and he veiled himself that we might find him only if we seek him. Of course, the downside of this gift is that people were given the ability to reject God, to turn away from what is good. Sadly we see the result of this rejection throughout the world. Chaos, suffering, evil, and darkness often mar what God had intended.

Yes, evil and suffering are problematic for us, but they are set alongside the other things we experience as humans: joy, compassion, love, and similar things that speak powerfully to us of those aspects of the world that God originally intended. Furthermore, we have to focus on the fact that we find evil and darkness disordered, and that we want to put right the things that we find wrong. This sense of disorder suggests that we have within us an understanding of how the world would have been had man not chosen to walk from God.

10. Even if the misuse of free will explains some human suffering, why do animals and the natural world suffer if God is good?

We never say that God actually wants suffering, but that he permits it for some purpose that is not, according to the Bible, his original plan. God may allow suffering to bring out heroism, to purify us, or simply to help remind us that there are realities beyond this world, beyond this created order. One useful image that can help us in understanding this problem of evil is when we look at the canvas of a masterpiece and we go right up to it: we only see blotches and brushstrokes; it looks all very unpleasant. We step a little bit away from it and suddenly it takes on form and texture. Then we stand at the requisite distance and suddenly we see its form, the complete picture. At least some of the suffering in this world can be seen from this broader perspective: it has a short sell-by date; it will not last forever. When we look at it later, with hindsight, we see that there is meaning in those blotches, in those brushstrokes, in what looks meaningless close up.

11. Some suffering may have a larger and good purpose, but surely a lot of suffering, like bad toothache, is just pointless and unpleasant?

As well as the problem of evil and suffering there's also the problem of stubbornness in our own natures. We don't do what we're meant to do even for our own good, a failure that is one consequence of what we call **ORIGINAL SIN**. We are born in a state of spiritual stubbornness: we don't do the things that we know that we ought to do, and we often do the things that we know we should not do; and we won't say sorry; and we won't listen when we're meant to;

12. Surely we need to be stubborn and look out for ourselves?

For the **Answers to Questions** turn to pages 49-50.

Can we know God and attain divine power to solve human problems by ourselves?

On the left are the ruins of the Parthenon of Athens, dedicated to the goddess Athena. At the centre is an image of Osiris, usually identified as the Egyptian god of the dead. On the right is part of the Aztec calendar stone, probably with the figure of Tonatiuh, the Aztec deity of the sun, who demanded human sacrifice as tribute.

The laborious construction of temples, often at the hearts of the great ruins of antiquity, witnesses not only to a yearning for divine interventions, but also to the need of societies to have a focal point or anchor point for peace and security. Various responses to these needs are at the root of much of the religious diversity of the world, both ancient and modern. Nevertheless, the pagan understanding of our relation to the divine tends to be one of supplicant to patron, and there is little of what is today called personal or second-person relatedness to the God of creation, let alone divine love and friendship. For example, the Greek philosopher Aristotle said that God is good, perfect and eternal, yet he never addressed God as 'you' and he claimed that friendship with God was impossible.

When human beings have attempted by themselves to bridge the separation of the human and the divine, they have tended to transfer the worship of God to contingent spiritual beings and to bestow flawed human or even bestial characteristics onto these 'gods', especially in carvings and other representations. In ancient cultures, these practices generated irrational and chaotic spiritual jungles often with obscene elements, some aspects of which have re-appeared in modern neo-pagan spiritualist movements. In its darkest form, ancient pagan worship was also characterised by human sacrifice, out of fear, to gods represented by monstrous and bestial images of terror.

Whatever else they produce, pagan practices have tended to do little in the long run to foster goodness, compassion or any hope of solving the deepest and most enduring human problems of sin and death. Even the pyramids of Egypt, vast tombs that were constructed to provide perpetual memorials for kings, are gradually crumbling back into the desert. Moreover, although all human beings seek happiness, neither ancient paganism nor the priorities of modern consumer culture offer convincing accounts of what happiness is and how it can be achieved. In his *Inferno* (canto IV), the poet Dante highlighted the way in which even ancient pagan visions of an afterlife, such as the Elysian Fields, have a spiritual emptiness about them, even if they are depictions of paradise.

The pyramids of the necropolis of Giza in Egypt, on the left, and the Elysian Fields, as depicted by Arthur Davies, on the right.

and we won't obey good people who give us advice. All this stubbornness is part of the legacy that we're born with. We call this legacy 'original sin'.

The Bible tells us the story of Adam, meaning 'every man', and Eve and the garden: of those who rejected God, who chose to worship self in place of him. We are taught that their disobedience has marred the human race, that each one of us contains within us a disordered desire. We are broken. Without **GRACE** our natural condition is to lean towards what is damaging, what is not good. We have no **REDEMPTION** through our own strength. We need the love of God if we are to overcome what is faulty within us.

13. Isn't the story of Adam and Eve just a pious myth, disproved by modern science?

Original sin can be understood as the first **SIN**, the sin of Adam and Eve, which was of disobedience. Original sin can also be understood as the loss of an inheritance. God gave to our ancestors, Adam and Eve, a particular inheritance of divine life which we call 'grace'. God also gave to our ancestors a harmonised human nature: a nature that was not inclined to sin. By that first sin, a rupture took place in the human race. Since then we all experience a tendency towards sin, and this tendency follows on from original sin.

14. If Adam and Eve sinned, why do we all have to suffer the consequences?

Is there hope?

To believe that there must be a God is a far cry from following a distinct religion. A first cause seems very distant from us, and yet people still seem to want to know more about this ultimate principle. Is this a possibility or a fantasy? Many acknowledge a thirst for God and yet there seems to be an unbridgeable gap between us and the Almighty. Could this God have revealed himself through history?

15. Do people really thirst for God? Surely many are uninterested.

God exists: that is a fact of reason and logic. But it's not sufficient for mankind merely that God exists. We need to know him, to understand him. If he is our creator and all-knowing, all-wise, all-good and all-loving, then we would expect that he would, in some way, interact with his **CREATION**. In fact, of course, he does, every minute of every day. He does so without interfering with our free will, our ability to choose between good and evil, which is what makes us human - and also what makes us like God, since he

16. Why does God initially choose just one people rather than revealing himself to everyone?

For the **Answers to Questions** turn to pages 50-51.

What is the significance of the Jewish People?

When asked by King Louis XIV of France for a proof of God, the philosopher Blaise Pascal is reported to have replied, "Why the Jews, your Majesty, the Jews!" The continuous existence of this people is a living miracle in the world. The Jewish people form the oldest self-identifying family in the world, tracing their lineage back for more than three and a half millennia to one man, Abraham, whose grandson Jacob ('Israel') became the father of twelve sons, the heads of twelve tribes. The term 'Jew' derives from the fourth son of Jacob, Judah, who gave his name to the tribe and kingdom of Judah, the 'Southern Kingdom' of Israel (c. 930–587 BC) with its great temple built by King Solomon and its capital at Jerusalem. The earliest writings of the Jewish people are today the oldest complete books in existence, and their laws are the oldest continuously-observed laws. All the books of what is now called the 'Old Testament' are from the Jewish people. Despite facing irrational and even diabolical persecution, the most terrible in recent times being by the Nazis (the Holocaust or Shoah), this people has been extraordinarily fruitful. Even though the Jewish people constitute less than 0.2% of the world's population, they have included over 20% of its Nobel Prize laureates, including Niels Bohr and Albert Einstein.

Archaeological remains from the past three thousand years of Jewish history. On the left is a fragment of a stele with the inscription 'Beit David' ('House of David'), believed to refer to David (c. 1040–970 BC), the greatest king of the ancient Jewish people (1, 2 S; 1 K; 1 Ch). In the centre is the Taylor Prism (c. 591 BC), which records the siege of Jerusalem during the reign of King Hezekiah, an event also described in Isaiah 33, 36; 2 Kings 18:17; 2 Chronicles 32:9. On the right at the top is the 'Cyrus cylinder', an account of an edict of the king of Persia that corroborates the general narrative of Ezra 1:1-4, in which Cyrus invited some exiled Jews to return to their homeland to rebuild their temple in Jerusalem. This second temple lasted from c. 530 BC to AD 70, when it was destroyed during the sack of the city by the Romans. On the right at the bottom is part of the Western ('Wailing') Wall today, the last remnant of the ancient wall that surrounded the temple's courtyard.

In contrast with the pagans, for whom the one God was a distant 'unmoved mover', the Jewish people proclaimed that God had actively revealed himself, *"What great nation is there that has a god so near to it as the Lord our God is to us?"* (*Dt* 4:7). Although the divine name of God was too holy even to pronounce, the constant theme of Jewish history was a covenant, almost a spiritual marriage, between the one God and his chosen people. Hence the greatest command of the Jewish law was, *"Hear, O Israel: The LORD our God is one LORD; and you shall love the LORD your God with all your heart, and with all your soul, and with all your might"* (*Dt* 6:4-5). All other commandments of the law, including the Ten Commandments, were consequences of this command, especially the rejection of the many gods of ancient paganism, worship of which was considered spiritual adultery. Nevertheless, although the Jews recognised that their covenant brought them closer to God, they regarded it as impossible to see the face of God (*Ex* 33:22). Moreover, they failed to stay completely faithful to the covenant and their history was marked by suffering, war and long periods of exile.

has the ability to choose. So he reveals himself to us little by little, which he has done throughout history, particularly to the **JEWISH** people whom he chose as the people to whom he would first reveal himself and some of his teachings.

As a consequence of this revelation of himself, a great characteristic of the Jewish people and their religion is that they believe in a **MESSIAH**, the Anointed One ('Christ').

A very strong sense that comes into the history of the Jewish people is the sense that God has become present to his people: that he has become close to his people and that they are close to him. In fact this became the central theme of the Jewish people. When they worried about **DEATH**, they did not worry so much about their own physical death as fear the possibility that they might not be able to worship and **KNOW GOD** when they went down to the land of the dead. Their relationship with God became the greatest treasure of their history: they had come to love with God the things that God loves and to sacrifice with God the things that God sacrifices. This very close relationship to God is described in the history of the Jewish people. There is a series of covenants that express this relationship - the nearest equivalent of this relationship we have in modern English is of a **MARRIAGE**. The covenant was a spiritual marriage of God with his people.

17. If God was uniquely close to the Jewish people, why did they suffer so much?

What we call the **OLD TESTAMENT** of the Bible, the Hebrew **SCRIPTURES**, are ancient texts. When you set faith aside and look at them fairly and squarely, you realise that they give us incredible insights into the relationship between God and the human person, between humanity and the divine. They tell us that God has come in search of us, that he has wanted to reveal himself to us, to save us and to draw us out of our misery. The Bible gives us stages of real events in history when he first of all forms one family in **ABRAHAM** and then, under **MOSES**, he gives a law to establish a people and a land. Then he builds up a kingdom with **DAVID**, the circles of God's influence growing ever wider and wider. And then he sends **PROPHETS** to promise that a saviour would come who would give a light for the entire world. His plan is recorded in this incredible book of history that we call the Bible, and that series of books that we call the Old Testament.

18. Don't experts tell us that much of what is written in the Bible is untrustworthy since it is wrong, of dubious origin, or distorted by people with agendas?

For the **Answers to Questions** turn to page 51.

What was the hope of the Jewish People?

Moses striking water from the rock by Nicolas Poussin

The scene above portrays the accounts of Exodus 17:1-7 and Numbers 20:2-13, part of the narrative of the liberation of the people of Israel from slavery in Egypt and their journey, under the leadership of Moses, to their promised land. During their long wandering in the wilderness, God commanded Moses to strike a rock from which water flowed to quench the thirst of the people. Much later, this journey and its miracles were seen as having additional spiritual meanings, including the journey of a human soul through the wilderness of this life towards a new and eternal life with God in a blessed kingdom.

The Old Testament is a narrative with an unfinished story. These books witness to acts of God in history that established a unique relationship with the Jewish people. To Noah, God promised to preserve the world from destruction, giving humanity the opportunity to be saved. To Abraham, God promised descendants and a new land. To Moses, God also promised a new land and gave a law for his chosen people (c. 1450 or 1250 BC). To King David, God promised that his descendant would reign over a kingdom that had no end (c. 1000 BC). By various prophets, such as Elijah, Isaiah, Jeremiah and Ezekiel (c. 900–400 BC), God promised that there would be a new covenant and a final salvation from the most deadly enemies of humanity: sin and death. God also promised that this salvation would come about by means of a saviour, an 'anointed one', a translation of the word 'messiah' or 'Christ'. Finally, in c. AD 20, a new prophet called John appeared in the wilderness of Judea with the message, *"Repent, for the kingdom of heaven is at hand"* (Mt 3:2).

Anna and the Blind Tobit by Rembrandt

Tobit, who remained faithful to God despite his suffering, is also a symbol in the Old Testament of the Jewish people awaiting the Messiah (Christ).

The story of the Old Testament is really very simple: it speaks of the Fall of man - how we lost our relationship with God and found ourselves alone with no hope of redemption. God, because he loved us so much, then sent prophets to call us back, to bring us into relationship with him once more. Again and again, we refused to listen. We even killed the prophets he sent. But time and again we also heard that God had a plan: that he would send into the world a saviour, a messiah who would undo the sin of Adam and restore **Heaven**.

19. Don't the people in the Old Testament also do a lot of killing at God's command?

For the **Answers to Questions** turn to page 51.

THE TEN COMMANDMENTS

The privileged expression of the natural moral law revealed by God to Moses:

1. **I am the Lord your God: you shall not have strange gods before me.**
   You shall not have strange gods before me. You shall not make to thyself any graven thing; nor the likeness of anything that is in heaven above, or in the earth beneath, nor of those things that are in the waters under the earth. You shall not adore them nor serve them.

2. **You shall not take the name of the Lord your God in vain.**

3. **Remember to keep holy the Lord's Day.**

4. **Honour your father and your mother.**

5. **You shall not kill.**

6. **You shall not commit adultery.**

7. **You shall not steal.**

8. **You shall not bear false witness against your neighbour.**

9. **You shall not covet your neighbour's wife.**

10. **You shall not covet your neighbour's goods.**

THE SANCTUS PRAYER

Holy, Holy, Holy Lord God of hosts.
Heaven and earth are full of your glory.
Hosanna in the highest.
Blessed is he who comes in the name of the Lord.
Hosanna in the highest.

Did Jesus Christ really exist?
Do we have accurate accounts of his life and work?

Yes, Jesus Christ really existed. The life and work of Jesus Christ are probably better and more fully attested than that of any other person in the ancient world. We know about Jesus Christ principally by means of the twenty-seven documents called the New Testament, which include four narratives of his life, the Gospels of Matthew, Mark, Luke and John. The documents of the New Testament, written between approximately twenty and seventy years after his public ministry, constitute the largest volume of written evidence in the ancient world about any one person. Other early Christian works from the late first or early second century, such the First Epistle of Clement and the Didache (The Teaching of the Twelve Apostles), corroborate some details of Jesus' life and teaching. The two greatest non-Christian historians of the first century also confirm some basic facts: the Roman historian Tacitus states that Christ suffered the 'extreme penalty' under Pontius Pilate; the Jewish historian Josephus refers to Jesus, called 'the Christ', and to his trial by the Sanhedrin.

Along with many coins, the inscription on this block of limestone, discovered in 1961, refers to "Pontius Pilate, the prefect of Judaea." In his Annals 15.44, the Roman historian and senator Tacitus refers to Christ, his execution by Pontius Pilate and the existence of early Christians in Rome in AD 64, during the reign of Roman Emperor Nero.

The oldest known papyrus fragment of the New Testament, dating from c. AD 125–150. This fragment was discovered in Egypt in 1920 and is now at the John Rylands Library in Manchester. The text can be matched to John 18:31-33, part of the account of the trial of Jesus Christ.

Although the sources of the life of Jesus Christ use a variety of styles, details and arrangements, a single clear personality emerges. Moreover, there is no serious evidence that these sources were ever modified significantly. Papyrus fragments, such as the Rylands Papyrus 457 [P52] above, and many scriptural citations in the works of early Christian writers, such as St Justin Martyr in the mid-second century and Tertullian at the start of the third century, can be matched to texts of the New Testament today. Finally, two large physical manuscripts have survived from the fourth century that together cover nearly the entire New Testament: the *Codex Vaticanus* and the *Codex Sinaiticus*. The cumulative effect of these sources, together with intensive work in textual criticism over the past two centuries, gives us a high degree of confidence in the substantial integrity of the New Testament texts.

Why Christ?

Who is Jesus Christ?

CHRISTIANS believe that JESUS CHRIST is the centre of their lives and even claim to have found the meaning of life in him. But what do we know about him? What was his life and mission about? Why should Jesus Christ be trusted as a privileged voice amongst others?

1. Why is Jesus so special? Haven't there been many prophets and messiahs?

Through history God had been preparing the world for the coming of a solution - a saviour figure - and finally he arrived. At the high point of the Roman Empire, in the reign of Caesar Augustus, when the whole world was being counted and when the *Pax Romana* spread across the world, in a dusty outpost of the empire in what is known as Palestine, a baby was born, an obscure baby in a place of massive significance: a place called Bethlehem, a place that was filled with prophecies of old that a new King would arise to rule. Christians believe that this figure, also called Christ, the Anointed One, the King, the Messiah, was to be the solution for mankind - the bridge between heaven and earth, to free us from all our difficulties, helplessness and meaninglessness. This figure of Christ is central to all of history and time, and we still measure time by his coming. We use the phrase 'Anno Domini' (AD)", which does not mean 'after Christ' but 'in the year of the Lord', a phrase that expresses our belief that this figure is also God, that he still reigns.

2. If Jesus was sent by God, why was he so obscure when he was born?

The essential point that we need to understand about Christ is that he was the one who was promised: he is GOD'S WORD. God spoke his Word in Christ, the Word that became flesh and blood among us. Moreover, we can expect him to tell us who he is: he is GOD THE SON; he and the FATHER are one; access to the Father is through him. Christ can also perform miracles: he can walk across water; he can multiply bread and fish. And we understand that everything he teaches is because we need the answer to the question the apostles asked when he calmed the storm, *"Who can this be, that even the winds and the sea obey him?"* (*Mt* 8:27) This is the one who was promised: that is the essence of his teaching.

3. Does the Bible actually say that Jesus is God and that he claimed to be God?

For the **Answers to Questions** turn to page 52.

How did Jesus come to be born?

The following text is a passage from the beginning of the gospel of Luke that describes the annunciation of the birth of Jesus. This Gospel is introduced as a narrative drawn from eyewitness accounts of the life of Christ, who was born in the days of Herod, king of Judea (cf. *Lk* 1:1-5).

> *"In the sixth month the angel Gabriel was sent from God to a city of Galilee named Nazareth, to a virgin betrothed to a man whose name was Joseph, of the house of David; and the virgin's name was Mary. And he came to her and said, 'Hail, full of grace, the Lord is with you!' But she was greatly troubled at the saying, and considered in her mind what sort of greeting this might be. And the angel said to her, 'Do not be afraid, Mary, for you have found grace with God. And behold, you will conceive in your womb and bear a son, and you shall call his name Jesus. He will be great, and will be called the Son of the Most High; and the Lord God will give to him the throne of his father David, and he will reign over the house of Jacob for ever; and of his kingdom there will be no end.' And Mary said to the angel, 'How shall this be, because I know not man?' And the angel said to her, 'The Holy Spirit will come upon you, and the power of the Most High will overshadow you; therefore the child to be born will be called holy, the Son of God.'"* Lk 1:26-38

The Adoration of the Shepherds by Bartolomé Esteban Murillo (c. 1650)

The artist has drawn together many themes from the Gospels, the narratives of the life of Jesus Christ in the Bible. We are told that Jesus was born in the reign of the Roman Emperor Caesar Augustus, probably between 6 and 4 BC ('Before Christ') by our present dating system. Jesus was born in poverty in the town of Bethlehem in Judea, where Mary laid him in a manger for cattle, because there was no room at the inn (*Lk* 2:7). The artist depicts the shepherds who had seen a vision of angels announcing the birth of Christ and who came to Bethlehem to see the child (cf. *Lk* 2:1-21). The ox and the ass on the left refer to the prophecy of Isaiah, *"The ox knows its owner, and the ass its master's crib"* (*Is* 1:3). The lamb on the right foreshadows the future sacrificial death of Jesus, who is also called the 'Lamb of God' by John the Baptist (*Jn* 1:29).

A miracle is an action where the effect must be through divine power. JESUS performed many miracles, not by praying that somebody else would perform one, but simply by ordering that these miracles be done. For example, he cast out demons and quieted a storm. Jesus did these miracles out of his own power, a revelation that he has divine power and that he is God.

Jesus demonstrates miracles regarding the whole of creation. He shows power over inanimate things like water and wind by calming the storm. He clearly has power over plants and trees: he curses the fig tree and it stops producing figs. He also has power over man: we see this from the fact that he forgives sins and that he heals leprosy and other illnesses.

4. Jesus may have worked miracles two thousand years ago, but why can't we see spectacular signs of his power today?

When looking at the miracles of healing to do with forgiveness, people were astonished and even angry, "How can anyone forgive sins? Who can forgive sin but God alone?" Christ is saying, in effect, "Yes, listen to me!" He is revealing, very gently, who he is and what he claims to do. So Christ's miracles were astonishing but they also communicated a message at another level, and you can still feel the astonishment when you read the stories today.

5. What is a 'sin', and why would I need anyone else to forgive my sins?

Some people say, "How do you trust these texts? They are two thousand years old!" The key to this trust is that they're written by eyewitnesses. We have more evidence about Jesus than virtually any other person in the ancient world. We have twenty-seven documents written by his followers with different perceptions and ideas. Also, secular writers speak about him: Josephus the Roman-Jewish historian and Tacitus the Roman chronicler. They tell us about the reality of this figure called Jesus, called *Christus* or Christ.

6. How do we know these texts have not been corrupted or altered for propaganda?

Jesus begins his ministry working great signs. He changes water into wine to help a couple at their wedding feast when they run out of wine. He shows his divine power by healing the sick, by curing the disorders of the soul and by working great miracles in nature. All these things are done to point towards something even more extraordinary that is gradually revealed in the GOSPELS. Because although Jesus is working great signs and teaching extraordinary truths that have never been heard before, the central part of his message is in fact himself. He is described as the Way, the Truth, and the Life (*Jn* 14:6): that is the extraordinary thing. He is the way to God; he is the truth about God - and when we say the word 'truth' we mean a

7. How can a person be a message, or a 'word' (of God or anything else)?

For the **Answers to Questions** turn to pages 52-53.

What did Jesus Christ teach us?

The period during which Jesus was a public figure was astonishingly brief: probably no more than three and a half years, c. AD 24–27. Much of his recorded teaching is in the form of short stories called parables. A theme of many parables, such as The Bridesmaids (*Mt* 25:1-13), and discourses like The Sheep and the Goats (*Mt* 25:31–46), is that our earthly lives are a brief period that enables us to change and be fruitful. What we become by the end of this life determines our judgement to eternal life or eternal death. The Parable of the Sower (*Mk* 4:3-20; *Lk* 8:5-15) also teaches us that our eternal fruitfulness in heaven does not depend on our natural abilities, but the manner in which we receive God's word. This word of God is not a 'word' in the usual sense, but a person: Jesus himself (*Jn* 1:1). Jesus taught that, *"I am the way, and the truth, and the life; no one comes to the Father, but by me."* (*Jn* 14:6)

The four Gospels also describe Jesus working a great variety of miracles: physical cures, the casting out of evil spirits, resurrections from the dead and control over nature. The latter include turning water into wine at a wedding, great catches of fish, the feeding of thousands by multiplication of loaves and fish, walking on water, calming a storm, and being transformed into a figure of brilliant radiance and glory.

The Sermon on the Mount by Carl Heinrich Bloch, depicting Christ's teaching on ethics and discipleship in Matthew 5-7, *"Be perfect, as your heavenly Father is perfect"* (*Mt* 5:48).

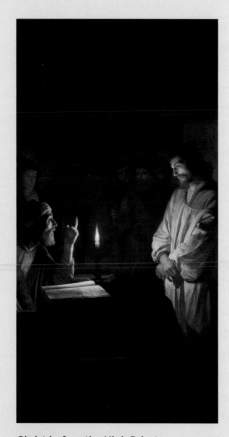

Christ before the High Priest by Gerrit van Honthorst

In the Parable of the Unfaithful Tenants, Jesus indicates his relationship to God the Father:

> *"Then the owner of the vineyard said, 'What shall I do? I will send my beloved son; it may be they will respect him.' But when the tenants saw him, they said to themselves, 'This is the heir; let us kill him, that the inheritance may be ours.'"* Lk 20:13-14

By this parable, in which the 'vineyard' is the world and the 'owner' is God the Father, Jesus teaches that he is not merely a prophet but the Beloved Son (cf. *Mt* 11:27; *Mk* 12:6). While some accepted Jesus as the Son of God and Son of Man, many wanted to kill him for blasphemy. When he affirmed his identity as the Christ, the Son of the living God, before the High Priest (cf. *Mk* 14:61-62), he was condemned to death, fulfilling his prophecy that his mission – to bring us eternal life – would bring him a cruel death by crucifixion.

> *"The high priest asked him, 'Are you the Christ, the Son of the Blessed?' And Jesus said, 'I am; and you will see the Son of man seated at the right hand of Power, and coming with the clouds of heaven.'"* Mk 14:61-62

correspondence with reality. So he corresponds perfectly with God because he is God; and he also corresponds perfectly with us because he is one of us, a man born of a woman, MARY. And so he is a kind of bridge between God and ourselves.

Jesus asked his DISCIPLES, *"Who do people say I am?"* He would reveal the answer to that question stage by stage. He revealed that he was in a unique and eternal timeless relationship with the Father. He also revealed that there was a HOLY SPIRIT who was related to him and the Father in eternity and whom he would send to this world. He said shocking things like, *"I saw Satan fall from heaven like lightning"* (*Lk* 10:18) and, *"Before Abraham was, I Am"* (*Jn* 8:58), when Abraham had existed two thousand years previously. By his miracles - his miracles over nature, his healings, the fact that he forgave sins, which is a prerogative of God - he showed us he was no ordinary man, nor a mere SAINT, nor just a great prophet or a king. He was God enfleshed. That is the key Christian belief, that the eternal God is not just one person but three divine persons; and the Son, the eternal Word of God, became a human being, entered into flesh and dwelt amongst us, literally and physically uniting God and man, heaven and earth.

8. If Jesus is God, and his Father is God, and the Spirit is God, are there three gods?

Why did Jesus die?

Even if Jesus Christ is someone absolutely unique, why do Christians think he is so important and what difference does he make to the world?

9. Is it not beneficial to draw from all kinds of spiritual traditions?

Some of the strongest evidence that Christ really meant to claim that he was the Son of God comes from the reaction of his adversaries. He was arrested and brought before the High Priest, who asked him, *"Are you the Christ, the Son of the Blessed One?"* (*Mk* 14:61) This phrase is an interesting use of language because the Jewish people knew that God is holy and so they never used God's name, but always referred to God indirectly, such as the 'Blessed One' or the 'Holy One'.

10. If God can do anything, why was Christ needed to end our separation from God?

Christ said, *"I am,"* and with that very phrase he is condemned to death because he is assumed to be speaking blasphemy, but for Christ it is not blasphemy, because for Christ alone it is true. He is the only begotten Son of God. So Jesus Christ was given up to a shameful death, crucified by the Romans, the worst and most ignominious death the Romans could devise.

For the **Answers to Questions** turn to pages 53-54.

How did Jesus Christ die?

Christ Crucified by Bartolomé Esteban Murillo

Jesus was arrested in the Garden of Gethsemane outside the walls of Jerusalem. He was tried, found guilty and handed over to the Roman governor Pontius Pilate, who ordered him to be crucified. Jesus was scourged, crowned with thorns and led to the hill of Calvary carrying his own cross. While being crucified, he prayed, *"Father, forgive them; for they know not what they do"* (*Lk* 23:34). As he died he said, *"It is accomplished"* (*Jn* 19:30). Artistic depictions of the crucifixion often show a skull below or at the base of the cross: this skull symbolises Adam, the good news being that the blood shed by the second Adam, Christ, has redeemed the sins of the first Adam and his descendants.

By this death, God has given over his only begotten Son as a sacrifice and gradually what emerges from Scripture is that this sacrifice is for us. This sacrifice is to save us from our sins.

We are told that when Jesus died on the cross, there was an extraordinary sign: there was an earthquake and the veil of the TEMPLE was torn in two (*Mt* 27:51). The veil of the Temple separated the human race from the Holy of Holies. Behind the veil of the Temple was the place of God's presence, and, with the veil of the Temple torn, that was a symbol that the separation between God and human beings had been ended. The unthinkable gap between human beings and God had been bridged by the person of Christ and by the sacrifice of Christ on the cross.

The crucifixion arises because Christ comes to teach, and, because of sin and evil, he is rejected. He is falsely accused, falsely tried, falsely condemned, and falsely put to death. But he allows these things to happen to him for a number of reasons. First, because by this sacrifice he makes up in his own person, being God, for all the evil in the world. Second, these deeds leave an example to us, showing that we have to participate in accepting the difficulties of this life, using him as our exemplar, and so save ourselves by co-operating with Christ and with his particular sacrifice, which was the crucifixion. If you consider Jesus wasn't just a man like Socrates being put to death unjustly by the state, but God himself, then you begin to understand the significance of this particular sacrifice, the crucifixion, and why it is central to Christianity and Christian teaching.

11. How can the cruel death of an innocent man, let alone of God himself, take sin away rather than curse the world still more?

Jesus lays down his life: he knows he must do that and he does it freely, but it is very hard to understand why. Why did he have to die on the cross? In response, he tells us that his death is so that we may have life, *"I have come that they may have life, and have it to the full"* (*Jn* 10:10), and *"When I am lifted up, I will draw all to myself"* (*Jn* 12:32). That cross is going to be the bridge between heaven and earth: it is to take away all the sin, misery, suffering, all the separation of humanity and God - all in that act of love - because he offers his life as an innocent with the infinite power of God, whom he is. He lays down his life and this death reverses everything.

12. How can a cross, an instrument of torture and death, bring anyone to life or heaven?

For the **Answers to Questions** turn to page 54.

What happened after Jesus died?

The four Gospels and the letters of St Paul in the New Testament, notably 1 Corinthians 15:3-8, testify that Jesus Christ rose from the dead. All four Gospels state that the tomb was found empty on the morning after the sabbath and relate a variety of encounters with the risen Jesus. In Luke 24:36-43, Jesus invites his disciples to touch him to see that he is not a ghost, and he eats a piece of fish in front of them. In John 20:25-28, the disciple Thomas says that he will not believe in the resurrection unless he sees Jesus and actually touches the wounds of the crucifixion. Jesus appears and invites Thomas, *"Put your finger here, and see my hands; and put out your hand, and place it in my side; do not be faithless, but believing."* Thomas answers him, *"My Lord and my God!"* 1 Corinthians 15:4-6, probably written c. AD 53–57, states that, *"He [Jesus] appeared to Cephas [Peter], then to the twelve. Then he appeared to more than five hundred brethren at one time, most of whom are still alive."*

Examples of encounters with the risen Christ

"Jesus said to her, 'Mary!' She turned and said to him, 'Rabboni!' (which is to say, teacher). Jesus said to her, 'Do not cling to me, for I have not yet ascended to the Father.'" Jn 20:16

The Appearance of Christ to Mary Magdalene by Alexander Ivanov

"When he was at table with them, he took the bread and blessed, and broke it, and gave it to them. And their eyes were opened and they recognised him; and he vanished out of their sight." Lk 24:30-35

Supper at Emmaus by Caravaggio

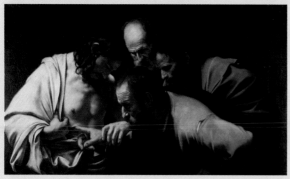

"Jesus came and stood among them, and said, 'Peace be with you.' Then he said to Thomas, 'Put your finger here, and see my hands; and put out your hand, and place it in my side; do not be faithless, but believing.' Thomas answered him, 'My Lord and my God!'" Jn 20:26-28

The Incredulity of Saint Thomas by Caravaggio

In summary, the fact of Christ's resurrection is attested by more than five hundred eyewitnesses, of upright life, who had nothing in this life to gain but everything to lose by their testimony. Moreover, although those opposed to Christ and the resurrection could have discovered deception easily, had there been any, they could give no answer except to threaten the apostles (*Ac* 4:17). The thousands and then millions, both Jews and Gentiles, who believed the testimony of the apostles in spite of the disadvantages of following such a belief, is also indirect evidence for the resurrection.

We need to understand this is not some sort of horrible bargain. This is all about love. God loved us so much that he came and joined us and died for us. This isn't a bargaining, "I will take your sins and if I suffer enough will that work?" This sacrifice is all to do with the pouring out of love. Jesus shed his blood for us because he loved us, and there is a sense in which we too share in his suffering. Indeed, we know in our lives and in the wider world that everything is bound up with what happened to Christ on the cross. Christ's love for us was so great that his offering was not just a question of words or loving deeds, it was the whole of himself. He gave himself to torture and death. And among much more, this sacrifice also means that whatever happens to us - our suffering, our humiliation, our being misunderstood, everything - has got some kind of deep meaning. Nothing is without value. The cross is at the vortex of everything and it is cosmically significant. It means something individually, personally - something to you and to me.

13. If following Christ means suffering and rejection, why is the gospel 'good news' of happiness and joy?

What hope does Jesus bring?

Religion is a very personal matter, and Jesus Christ's coming seems historically important. But what impact does he have on my life and on the challenges that I face?

14. How is it that many people manage to live well and cope with challenges without Christ?

If the Gospels ended on the cross, with Jesus Christ simply dying, then death would have the final laugh. We would have had the story of the most wonderful human teacher ending in the grave. But no, God triumphed, death lost its sting, and Christ was raised to heaven, pointing us to where we can follow. Death need hold us back no more. The whole point and purpose of the RESURRECTION is to destroy the order of death and lead us to the gospel of life everlasting.

15. Why do we still have to die if Christ has conquered death?

We are told that, after three days, Jesus Christ rose from the dead. We are given various accounts that convey the physicality of this event. For example, Jesus invites his disciples to see for themselves by showing them his hands and his sides. Of course, what's so extraordinary about this invitation is that his hands were pierced by the nails by

16. If Christ had the power to rise from the dead, why was he left still wounded?

For the **Answers to Questions** turn to pages 54-55.

What gifts did Christ leave us?

Christ's gifts to us include much more than his teaching. By means of his ministry, death and resurrection, he offers us forgiveness of sins and a new kind of life, *"I came that they may have life, and have it abundantly"* (*Jn* 10:10). This life is described as partaking in the divine nature (*2 P* 1:4), by which we become co-heirs of Christ (*Rm* 8:17) and temples of God's Holy Spirit (*1 Co* 3:16), able to call God 'Our Father' (*Mt* 6:9; *Lk* 11:2). This new life, also called the life of grace, brings about a supernatural friendship with God, enabling us to approach God with awe but also with intimacy and love (*Heb* 4:16). The life of grace begins in this world but does not end with our physical death. If we die in a state of grace, then our souls will one day be with God in heaven and, at the general resurrection, our bodies will be glorified forever, just as Christ has been raised and will never die again. The sacraments, established by Christ and enacted through sacred rites, plant, nourish and restore grace in us.

The Sacrament of Baptism

Jesus said, *"Truly, truly, I say to you, unless one is born of water and the Spirit, he cannot enter the kingdom of God"* (*Jn* 3:5). This second birth as an adopted child of God is called 'baptism': the ordinary way of salvation for every human being and the beginning of the Christian life of grace. Christ was himself baptised, he baptised others (*Jn* 3:22) and commanded his disciples to baptise, *"In the name of the Father, and of the Son, and of the Holy Spirit"* (*Mt* 28:19), in other words, in the name of the three persons of God (the Trinity).

The Sacrament of the Eucharist

On the evening before his death, Jesus took bread and wine and said, *"Take this, all of you, and eat it, for this is my Body, which will be given up for you...this is the chalice of my Blood, the Blood of the new and eternal covenant, which will be poured out for you and for many for the forgiveness of sins."* Jesus added, *"Do this in memory of me,"* instituting the sacrifice and sacrament of the Eucharist, by which his body, his blood and the saving power of his death are made present, nourishing the life of grace.

Five other sacraments have been given to us. The institution of the Sacrament of Confession bestowed Christ's authority to forgive sins on his apostles, *"If you forgive the sins of any, they are forgiven; if you retain the sins of any, they are retained"* (*Jn* 20:23). The Sacrament of Confirmation seals a person with the Holy Spirit for the mature Christian life (cf. *Ac* 2) and the Sacrament of Anointing forgives sins and strengthens the soul, especially during serious illness or at the approach of death, to heal people or to help them die in a state of grace (cf. *Jm* 5:14-15). The Sacrament of Holy Orders ordains a man to act in the person of Christ, giving rise to the threefold ministry of deacon, priest and bishop to teach, govern and sanctify God's people. Matrimony raises the natural marriage of a man and woman to the dignity of a sacrament (*Ep* 5:31-32; cf. *Jn* 2).

In a good Christian life, these sacraments act on our human nature to plant, nurture and restore the life of grace, cultivating holiness and friendship with God. Just as a seed is planted in the ground to grow and bear fruit, we are called by God to be spiritually fruitful with his gifts of grace. For those who die in the love of God, this fruitfulness will bless them in eternity (cf. *Rv* 14:13).

which he had been crucified - nailed to the cross - and in his side was the hole made by the soldier's spear, thrust into him to make sure he was dead. By showing them his hands and his side he was also showing them that he was the genuine Jesus Christ, the one they had known, the one that they had followed for three years, and that he had risen from the dead, triumphant over sin and death. He offers us the promise - not just of a restored life of the soul, which is the primary gift of the life of grace, but also the promise of a bodily resurrection; that God wants us one day to be raised body and soul in the glory of the kingdom of heaven, never to die again.

There is plenty of evidence for the resurrection: St Paul tells us that Jesus was seen by several hundred followers at one time, and there are accounts of individual eyewitnesses, all recorded in the NEW TESTAMENT and by early Christian writings. This event changed people; it changed huge numbers of people because people knew it was true. This was an event that had never happened before and it is of massive significance. Not only was Jesus resurrected, coming back to life as many people are in hospitals today for a few more years or hours of life; no, he came back to an existence, to a body that was now glorified, that was going to last forever. In this resurrection we see, we touch, our future; he promises us that there is life beyond the grave, that death is not the end. By rising from the dead, Jesus also confirms that all of his teaching is true, that it is not mere wishful thinking but factual, that God had really entered into the world through him. And when he returns to heaven, where Christians believe he still lives today, he shows us the future of our humanity. Jesus tells us that we shall rise as well, that our bodies and souls have a future, that our lives are not defined merely by a few years and hours in this world. Beyond this colourful universe there is a reality that will last forever: we call it heaven.

17. Why did Jesus Christ only appear to those who had known and followed him before his death, and why did many of them also fail to recognise him?

In the encounters recorded in the four Gospels, various groups of people see Jesus Christ raised from the dead. He appears to two disciples travelling to a town outside Jerusalem and actually walks along beside them. The disciples are talking about the crucifixion and Jesus begins explaining the significance of the Scriptures to them. It is extraordinary to consider that these disciples are talking about the death of Christ while Jesus is beside them, explaining the significance of his sacrifice and drawing from the prophecies made about it.

18. In many of these encounters Jesus suddenly appears or vanishes; doesn't that suggest that he was a ghostly projection?

For the **Answers to Questions** turn to page 55.

Christ's final commandment and promise

Christ the Consolator by Carl Bloch

Scripture describes Jesus ascending to heaven, bringing his glorified human nature into God's heavenly domain, establishing a new homeland and final place of rest for humanity (*Ac* 1:1-14). His last words to his disciples were, *"All authority in heaven and on earth has been given to me. Go therefore and make disciples of all nations, baptising them in the name of the Father and of the Son and of the Holy Spirit, teaching them to observe all that I have commanded you; and lo, I am with you always, to the close of the age"* (*Mt* 28:18-20). The leading disciples, called apostles, were also instructed to wait in the city of Jerusalem for a new gift, the Holy Spirit, that would inspire and bring to life a new community, established by God on earth to gather humanity to divine life in heaven. This work will continue until the end of time, when Jesus Christ will return to judge all of humanity. *"Behold, I am coming soon, bringing my recompense, to repay every one for what he has done. I am the Alpha and the Omega, the first and the last, the beginning and the end"* (*Rv* 22:12-13).

St Paul said quite starkly that if Christ is not raised, then your faith is in vain: you are still in your sins, and those who have died have perished. But Christ has been raised and this resurrection changes everything. Our hope is in him, in the promise that our sins, miseries, and sufferings can be taken away and that our relationships and our bodies have a future with him in heaven. This hope changes the way we look at the world; it changes everything. We know that apostles died for this message, that they were persecuted one way or another. St Peter was crucified in Rome, St Paul was decapitated, and St James was persecuted by King Herod. They died for the truth of their message, which is the greatest witness of its authenticity.

It is not enough simply to believe that these things happened two thousand years ago. Christianity is a living reality because Jesus Christ set up a body in this world to perpetuate his mission and to bring his power, through the gifts he gave to the world, to each age and to every place. And his last words on this earth were to go forth and teach all nations, *"Baptise them in the name of the Father and of the Son and of the Holy Spirit"*, and he said, *"I am with you till the end of the world"* (*Mt* 28:19-20).

19. Even if many followers of Jesus died for their faith, isn't that commitment found in many other kinds of religions, beliefs and cults?

For the **Answers to Questions** turn to page 55.

THE OUR FATHER

The great prayer that Jesus Christ taught his disciples, adopted as children of God through the grace of Baptism:

Our Father, who art in heaven,
hallowed be thy name;
thy kingdom come,
thy will be done
on earth as it is in heaven.
Give us this day our daily bread,
and forgive us our trespasses,
as we forgive those who trespass against us;
and lead us not into temptation,
but deliver us from evil.

Amen.

Where did the Church come from?

These are artistic representations of the biblical accounts of the origins of the Church. Pietro Perugino's painting above, *Christ Handing the Keys to St Peter*, depicts the scene in Matthew's Gospel 16:18-19 when Christ gives authority to Peter, the leader of the apostles, who were the first bishops of the Church, *"You are Peter, and on this rock I will build my church, and the gates of hell shall not prevail against it. I will give you the keys of the kingdom of heaven, and whatever you bind on earth shall be bound in heaven, and whatever you loose on earth shall be loosed in heaven."* The successors of St Peter, who was crucified in Rome on Vatican hill by the Emperor Nero in c. AD 64, are the bishops of Rome, who are also called the popes. Jean II Restout's painting below, *Pentecost*, depicts the scene in the Acts of the Apostles 2:1-4 when the Holy Spirit brings this new, supernatural community to life, and the mission of the Church begins to gather humanity to divine life in heaven.

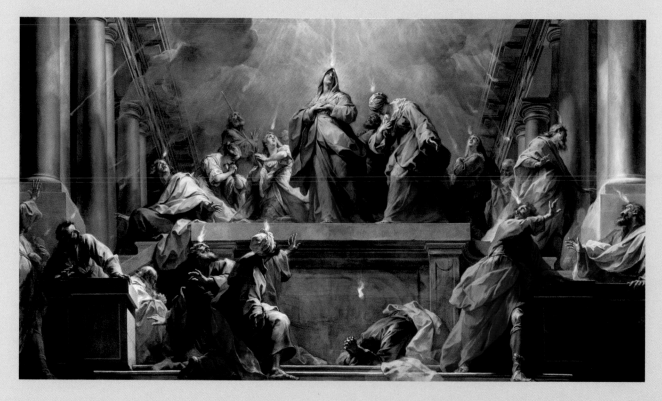

Why the Church?

What is the Church?

Did Jesus Christ really found a CHURCH as a bridge between the human family and God? What do CATHOLICS believe about the Church? What is the Church's real origin and why do so many oppose it?

The story of the Gospel of Christ does not end with Christ's death and resurrection. He understood that we would need much more than that to live the Christian life. And so before he died on the cross, he instructed his APOSTLES and established the Church to guide us, holding us as his family here on earth. After his death and resurrection, he sent the Holy Spirit on the members of the Church, that they would not be relying solely on their own strength but be fired by the grace of the Lord.

Jesus Christ changed the world forever. We say that he saved the world. He bridged the unbridgeable gap between God and man, and gave meaning and purpose to our lives, taking our miseries and turning them into joys. He gave us hope and he set into this world a body, a living reality, which we call the Church, to be his family. The aim of the Church is to draw all people back to God as he intended in the first place - all of humanity. The Church is the family of God.

When Jesus Christ walked this earth he chose to form a Church - a new, SUPERNATURAL society. He said to his leading disciple ST PETER, his Prime Minister, *"You are Peter, and on this rock I will build my church, and the gates of hell will not prevail against it. I shall give you the keys of the kingdom of heaven, and whatever you bind on earth shall be bound in heaven, and whatever you loose on earth shall be loosed in in heaven"* (Mt 16:18-19). Peter was to be the first POPE, the first leader of the Church and the other disciples were to be the first BISHOPS. From St Peter's time to our present age there is a complete continuity of these popes, like a golden chain that traverses history and unites us with the beginning of the Church.
This office has kept the family of God together in unity.

1. Isn't organised religion, including the Church, the source of much evil and best avoided?

2. Didn't the Catholic Church appear long after the time of Jesus Christ, an invention of later men of power like the Emperor Constantine?

3. Why do we need the Pope and the other bishops if we have the Bible and faith in Jesus Christ?

For the **Answers to Questions** turn to page 56.

Why is the Church 'Catholic'?

The ruins of the Flavian Amphitheatre in Rome, also called the Colosseum, the possible place of execution in c. AD 107 of St Ignatius, one of the first Christian bishops. During the sea voyage that took him to his death, St Ignatius wrote a letter (*Epistle to the Smyrnaeans*, 8) in which he used the Greek word "καθολικός" (Catholic), meaning 'universal', 'complete' and 'whole', to describe the church, *"Wherever Jesus Christ is, there is the Catholic Church."*

A Christian city has arisen in Rome since the fall of its ancient Empire. St Peter's Basilica, above, is built over the burial site of St Peter, one of the twelve apostles of Jesus and the first of the bishops of Rome, who was crucified by the Emperor Nero c. AD 64. To be a member of a local church in union with the Church of Rome and its bishop, also called the Pope, unites a person with the Catholic Church and its long and continuous history, stretching back through the centuries to Christ himself.

The Church is absolutely fundamental to Christianity because otherwise, quite rightly, people would ask, "What is your authority?" The ancient maxim of the law is *quo warranto* - by what authority do you say this? And that is a perfectly legitimate question to ask of Christians as well. So Christ didn't simply come, be crucified, resurrected and leave, because if he did, there would be no continuing authority by which his followers would teach. This is a crucial issue, because if you don't have an authoritative teacher in the form of the Church, particularly the Pope and bishops, then how can we be sure that what we have heard and read about the resurrection of Christ is true, and how can we know what it means?

4. The Church may claim to have authority, but what makes this claim at all credible?

The great birth of the Church is recorded in the Acts of the Apostles, which is a continuation of the Gospel of St Luke. The Acts of the Apostles describes what happened next, what Christians did after the resurrection of Jesus Christ. What they did next is the story of the Church, beginning with the feast of PENTECOST. We are told that the apostles and various disciples are gathered together with Mary, the mother of Jesus. We are told that they experience the sound of a rushing wind and they see a vision like tongues of fire that separate and come to rest on the heads of each of those present. And suddenly those present are transformed: they begin an extraordinary ministry of preaching. Many of them, just a few days before, had been hiding in fear. Now we are told that Peter, the leader, stands up in front of a crowd of thousands gathered into Jerusalem for the festival of Pentecost. He starts preaching to them about Jesus Christ, showing that Jesus is the Messiah and how he is the fulfilment of all the prophecies. When they ask how they can be saved, Peter tells them to be baptised and join the Church, the new ISRAEL, the new community founded on the twelve apostles, just like the twelve tribes of Israel. This event is the beginning of the Church's missionary activity, which continues to the present day.

5. The birth and early growth of the Church narrated here seems rapid and full of wonder. Why does Christianity seem to be in decline in some places today?

The Church is called 'Catholic', a word that has been used since the earliest times of Christianity. The term 'Catholic' is from a Greek word meaning 'universal'. The Church is universal because she lasts through time, and also because she spreads across the world. In every country of the world you find members of Christ's church - Catholics: one billion of them.

6. Aren't there many good Christians who are not Catholic?

For the **Answers to Questions** turn to pages 56-57.

What are some of the visible fruits of the Catholic faith?

Although the principal goal of the Church is supernatural, namely to save souls from sin and gather humanity to divine life in heaven, the Church casts the reflected light of that life over the whole earth (*Gaudium et Spes*, 40), enriching human experience in a great diversity of ways. Out of a vast array of rich contributions, a few examples are selected here. Since holiness has to be cultivated with a disciplined, regular life, the measurement of time and record keeping have long been important to Catholicism (top right). From the early Middle Ages, Church bells marked the passage of time and the first clocks with mechanical escapements (producing a characteristic 'tick-tock') were used in cathedrals, monasteries and town halls by c. 1200. Subsequent, highly complex clocks stimulated the development of mechanics and precision engineering. The Gregorian Calendar of 1582, an achievement of early modern astronomy and especially of members of the Jesuit order, is named after Pope Gregory XIII and now used worldwide. Monastic orders, dedicated to a life of prayer, developed methods for recording sung chant on parchment, techniques which led to the invention of staff notation and the 'ut-re-mi' (do-re-mi) mnemonic by the Benedictine monk Guido of Arezzo (d. 1003). These inventions were of incalculable significance for the preservation, teaching and development of music (top left). The experience of monastic living, combined with new intellectual energy and the early development of the Western legal system in the twelfth century, helped to give rise to the first universities, such as Paris, Oxford (bottom left), Cambridge and Padua. There were over fifty universities in Europe by the middle of the fifteenth century. The great scholars of the Catholic Middle Ages, such as St Thomas Aquinas (d. 1274, bottom right), continue to influence intellectual life and culture across the world to the present day.

What does the Church do?

For many, the Catholic Church is not considered a force for good in the world. Why do so many find the Church a credible witness today, and what has the Church really brought to the world?

7. Hasn't the Church held people back, intellectually and morally?

The Church was established by Christ: it was there, present among the early Christians; it has spread throughout the world and it is visible today. Most people in most countries have access to a particular building called a 'Catholic Church' and most people are aware of the infrastructure of the bishops, the priests, and of the Holy Father, the Bishop of Rome, also called the 'Pope'. The question might then be, "What's it all for? We know that the Church has this extraordinary history, that she is rooted in Scripture, but why did God establish her? What is she intended to do?" The short answer to that question is that the Church is established by God to gather humanity to divine life in heaven. So you might say that the task of the Church is to produce saints, to produce citizens of the new and heavenly Jerusalem, the Kingdom of Heaven.

8. If the Church aims to produce saints in heaven, why is it full of sinners?

The Church is there for SALVATION, to get us home, to get us to eternal life. She is the family of God, to bring us as a family back to God. That is the reason for the Church, and all the other dimensions of the Church relate to this mission. Jesus Christ gave the Church some amazing gifts called 'SACRAMENTS' and there are seven of them: for example, BAPTISM, by which we are born into the family of God; the Holy EUCHARIST or Communion, by which we are united with Christ and God; and CONFESSION, the Sacrament of Reconciliation, by which our sins are forgiven. These sacraments are powerful gifts that help the Church to save us.

9. Why do we need complex things like sacraments and rules? Isn't it enough to have faith in Jesus?

Some of the other evidences for Christianity, and Catholicism in particular, are its fruits, because if you want to see if anything works, then you see what it has done and whether it has been successful.

10. Hasn't the Church been the source of much evil as well as good in the world?

For the **Answers to Questions** turn to pages 57-58.

How has the Catholic faith inspired art?

Since the Catholic faith teaches that the Son of God became man, and material reality in the form of the sacraments has become capable of transmitting divine life, expressions of art that filter and represent material reality can also be holy. Perhaps the most famous of all frescoes is the ceiling of the Sistine Chapel (1508–1512), painted by Michelangelo and including the creation of Adam (above), the fall of man into sin, and the drama of salvation by Jesus Christ. Curtains of light filtered through stained glass windows, a development of Catholic civilisation from at least the eighth century, have included masterpieces such as the South Rose Window of Notre Dame Cathedral in Paris (below).

It is extraordinarily encouraging in many ways to look at the different fruits of Catholic civilisation through the ages, because we see a kind of natural outpouring of God's grace. We see these fruits, for example, in great works of art. Christian themes inspired most of the great art between AD 500 and AD 1500, and on into the modern era as well. The Church has generated architecture because we needed buildings that would house the Blessed Eucharist, the Body of Christ, buildings commensurate with this extraordinary commission. So Christians produced buildings like Canterbury Cathedral, the other great buildings of the Christian world, and a variety of architectural styles. The Church has also inspired music: the whole of the Western musical tradition comes out of Catholic Christianity and even our musical notation system came out of the monasteries. You can cite many other achievements: individual Catholics have become great philosophers, like St Thomas Aquinas and St Augustine. These philosophers taught us about free will, about the natural law and helped to develop the Western legal tradition. Even matters like the laws of war today are influenced by Catholic Christianity.

11. How can the Church take credit for human achievements that might have been accomplished anyway, or even better, without faith?

The Church is essentially very creative, and brings forth in people some of the most magnificent art, literature, music, stained glass that the world has ever known. Western civilisation, as nurtured by the Church, is mankind's highest achievement: just think of the glories of soaring architecture - Westminster Abbey, and so on; think of the most fabulous paintings, such as those of Michelangelo; think of the great deeds of heroism, such as the idea that you would lay down your life for somebody else because you wanted to make them well; or think of Mother Teresa going round Calcutta caring for the poorest of the poor. The Church has an ability to foster in her children great, beautiful and noble deeds, and this in the most unlikely ways in spite of poverty, war, famine and difficulty. For me, the fruits we have seen in our civilisation are a proof of the truth, beauty, and goodness of the Christian faith.

12. Hasn't the Church (and Western civilisation in general) damaged and ruined other cultures, as well as the environment?

The greatest fruits of the Church and the best examples of Catholics are the saints. The philosopher Aristotle would always say that to understand a species you have to look at its best examples; then you know what the species is supposed to be. If we look to the saints, those holy men and women, we see what the Catholic Christian is supposed to be when we get the faith right. G. K. Chesterton once said that Catholicism has not been tried and found wanting - it has not been properly tried.

13. Aren't many of the saints rather peculiar and extreme?

For the **Answers to Questions** turn to page 58.

How does someone become Catholic?

A person becomes a Catholic through baptism, conferred by immersion in water or by pouring water over the head, together with the proper form of words, *"I baptise you in the name of the Father, and of the Son, and of the Holy Spirit."* This baptism normally takes place at a font in a Catholic church, the minister of baptism normally being a bishop, priest or deacon. Baptism frees us from Original Sin, makes us children of God and members of the Catholic Church. For infants, their parents consent to their baptism on their behalf and promise to bring them up in the faith. Adults are normally baptised after a period of preparation, with the baptism itself often taking place during the Mass of Holy Saturday, when the Church celebrates the night of the resurrection of Jesus Christ from the dead.

Many Christians today, however, have been baptised outside the Catholic Church, especially in various Protestant communities formed over the last five centuries. Those who have been baptised validly are already Christians. As adults, they come into full communion with the Catholic Church by going to Confession, making a public profession of faith, often at a Sunday Mass, and receiving the sacraments of Confirmation and Communion. This public profession of faith is simply, *"I believe and profess all that the holy Catholic Church believes, teaches, and proclaims to be revealed by God."*

The sacraments of initiation: Baptism, Confirmation and Communion.

What life does the Church offer us?

There are many who believe in God and in Jesus Christ who find no need for a church. What difference do Catholics believe that the Church makes in their lives?

Often when people talk about the Church, they think about clergymen, but of course the Church is lay people. As John Henry Newman famously said, "THE LAITY? The Church would look pretty silly without them." That's you and me; ordinary people. We have a mission, or rather the Church is a mission. We are all meant to share this good news of Christ with our friends and neighbours and live it out in our everyday lives, at work, in the family and so on. We live the sacramental life: we are fed with Christ himself in the Eucharist and we can take our sins to God and have them forgiven in Confession. So there is a rich sacramental life which it is the laity's right to have, and that also provides the tools with which we can EVANGELISE others, sharing the good news with those around us.

A truly sad aspect of modern life is that many people literally do not know why they were born. They don't know why they're here, but the Christian knows why he or she is here: we are made in the image and likeness of God and are deeply loved by God. Those around us need to know that every individual person is truly, hugely loved by God: this information is theirs by right.

People ask the question, "What do Catholics do?" Well, by and large, Catholics do what many people do: they grow up, raise families, go to work and so on. But for those who are practising their faith seriously, praying and making use of the sacraments, there will be a different perspective on life. The ultimate goal of the life of a Catholic is not in this world but is as a preparation and pilgrimage towards the kingdom of heaven. That goal changes the way in which we relate to the world around us in many ways: we have a certain 'lightness of touch' and do not need to worry too much about building our permanent home in this world. People are often obsessed with acquiring all kinds of material goods, trying, for example, to obtain financial security, worrying about their health and so on. All these things are important, of course, but there is

14. Can't I live a good life without going to church?

15. Why does God want or need to send us out on mission, if he is all-powerful?

16. If we focus on heaven, doesn't that mean we neglect this world?

For the **Answers to Questions** turn to page 59.

How do I grow spiritually as a Catholic?

Receiving the life of grace in baptism is just the beginning of a process of spiritual growth that should continue throughout a person's whole life until death. Jesus taught parables, such as the parable of the sower, to teach us how we should grow and be spiritually fruitful:

> "Listen! A sower went out to sow. And as he sowed, some seed fell along the path, and the birds came and devoured it. Other seed fell on rocky ground, where it had not much soil, and immediately it sprang up, since it had no depth of soil; and when the sun rose it was scorched, and since it had no root it withered away. Other seed fell among thorns and the thorns grew up and choked it, and it yielded no grain. And other seeds fell into good soil and brought forth grain, growing up and increasing and yielding thirtyfold and sixtyfold and a hundredfold." Mk 4:3-9

Jesus later explained that this parable warns of three states in which a person receives the word of God but is not fruitful (*Mk* 4:14-20). In the case of the seeds falling along the path, the evil one (Satan) immediately comes and takes away the word which is sown in them. In the case of the seeds sown in rocky ground, they receive the word with joy but have no root and so fall away when persecution or trouble come. For those sown among thorns, the cares of the world, delight in riches and the desire for other things enter in and choke the word and it proves fruitless.

When the word of God does take root deeply and flourishes in a person's life, the effects are public as well as personal. Christ commands his followers to practise charity, especially the corporal and spiritual works of mercy. Catholics are also called to pray and work for a more truly Christian society that respects natural law, upholds the dignity of all people, is amenable to the sharing of the gospel and conducive to helping all people to follow their God-given vocations.

God produces all spiritual growth, but the various states of this parable suggest ways in which we can co-operate with grace and avoid what will damage or destroy our spiritual fruitfulness:

- Hold onto this gift of life by fulfilling at least the basic minimum of what is required as a Catholic, notably Mass on Sundays and other Holy Days, and Confession at least around the time of Easter (ideally more frequently).

- Put down deep roots, which typically includes: praying each day; studying the faith, its history and its traditions; and allowing the faith to penetrate deeply into our lives and actions.

- Avoid not only sin but also the many things in this life that can choke us spiritually by needlessly absorbing our time and energy without bearing fruit.

The Angelus, by Jean-François Millet, depicts Catholics working in the fields and praying at the sound of a church bell. This painting illustrates the call to holiness in all areas of life, as well as showing the way in which this holiness is not manufactured, but cultivated by daily prayers and a disciplined life.

a bigger perspective, and Catholicism provides this bigger perspective. At the end of the day, if the worst thing that could happen to you physically is that you die, even that is not the end of the world: we are told by the resurrection of Christ that the soul goes on and that we shall one day be raised from the dead. The important thing is not how long we live but how we live, and particularly how we die - how we enter eternity and our relationship with God at the moment of death.

The saints with all their variety from different ages, and with different occupations and gifts for the world each show us a glimpse of Christ and hence a glimpse of God. They are God's gift to the world, but he wants every human being to be a saint: that is his design. Saints are not just specially set apart from other people, but are children of God relating to God as he originally intended. This way of living is open to every single human being in God's plan for the Church.

17. Isn't everyone a child of God, not just saints or Christians generally?

One of the things that people don't understand about the Christian faith is that it is not a series of rules, but a striving for truth, beauty and goodness that echoes with what is in our hearts. When the Church speaks about moral issues - how we should live, how we should behave with one another, our relationships together and our individual striving for goodness - she is often speaking about natural law. She speaks about the way we were meant to be from the beginning, God's original plan for the human race. We actually understand this because we see, for example, in marriage, that we are made - biologically made - for one man and one woman bound in faithfulness for life, raising children. We actually understand this law in the deep core of our being. So the Church, when she speaks to us of the natural law, the principles of which are in harmony with our bond with God, she expresses what is already written in our hearts and that we know to be true.

18. Surely a lot of the Church's rules, especially in sexual matters, are out-of-date, bigoted or unequal?

Apart from the sacraments, it is daily PRAYER that is most important for the transformation of our souls. The ideal Catholic life is one of strong prayer, each and every day, by which we draw close to God, allowing him to work with us and through us, and to make us fruitful by his grace. So it is not what we do as Catholics that is important, but how close we are to Christ. God will do the doing. All we have to do, in one sense, is to co-operate with grace, and we have evidence from the lives of the saints that this co-operation is extraordinarily fruitful.

19. Why does God want us to pray if he knows what we need already?

For the **Answers to Questions** turn to pages 59-60.

What can we hope for?

The Last Judgement by Fra Angelico

The great Christian writer C.S. Lewis said that in this life we write the title page of what we are to be in eternity (*The Last Battle*, ch. 16). Scripture tells us that one day we shall be judged (*Heb* 9:27) and that God has set before us the choice of life or death (*Dt* 30:19). For those who have been faithful to Christ and fruitful in love, following the grace given to them, God promises a new heaven and a new earth, where every tear will be wiped away and where we shall be like God, for we shall see him as he is (*1 Jn* 3:2). The Church exists to bring us to this true homeland, to live with Christ and his saints forever. *"Blessed are those called to the Wedding Feast of the Lamb"* (*Rv* 19:9).

The Mystic Lamb by Van Eyck
A representation of the Church in the glory of heaven.

Being Catholic means being part of the greatest, most vibrant family on earth. The Catholic life is one of word and sacrament, of being present at the Mass, and of receiving the many graces that the Church has to offer. This life means being a sign of contradiction in this world, pointing always to the lord of life who guides and leads us.

20. What about all the Christians who are not members of the Church?

The mission of the Church is to draw all people to God and to communicate a message of hope that is ultimately quite simple, "God loves you, he brought you into this world and he died for you on the cross." It is very important to share this message and to be a part of the Church.

21. If the Church's message is simple, why are its liturgies, doctrines, laws and practices so very complicated?

God who revealed himself in Christ wants us not only to know that heaven and earth have been bridged, but that we can cross that bridge to be with God. Heaven is our home and he wants us to get home. The Church does not simply bring light to humanity, although she has brought incredible gifts to civilisation. Her ultimate aim is human salvation, to bring us to God as his sons and daughters. That is the meaning of the Faith.

22. Surely it is arrogant to claim that the Church brought light to humanity. Wasn't the Enlightenment, which made the modern world, opposed by the Christian faith?

For the **Answers to Questions** turn to page 60.

THE HAIL MARY

The great prayer for the intercession of the Mother of Jesus Christ, who is glorified body and soul in heaven and who is the image and beginning of the Church in the world to come:

**Hail, Mary, full of grace,
the Lord is with thee;
blessed art thou among women,
and blessed is the fruit of thy womb, Jesus.**

**Holy Mary, Mother of God,
pray for us sinners, now,
and at the hour of our death.**

Amen.

Answers to Questions

Why God?

1. Why should I care if God exists or not?

The question of God's existence is important for anyone with an enquiring mind, in other words anyone who asks the question "Why?" The question of God's existence is also important from a human perspective because of our inability, without divine help, to find ultimate, true and lasting happiness when confronted with the problems of sin, suffering and death. As the philosopher Blaise Pascal argued, if we have to bet with our lives either that God exists or does not exist, then the possible gain from betting on the truth of the God's existence infinitely outweighs any loss from being wrong (*Pensées* § 233).

2. Surely the universe just *is*? We don't need to know anything else to explain it.

If we cease thinking of the universe as a single 'thing' but rather as the totality of all particular things – such as atoms, forces, dust, clouds, stars, plants, animals, minds, and so on – we cannot avoid asking for a cause of this totality if we have a desire to know anything properly at all, for none of these particular things cause themselves. Moreover, why should we investigate the causes of some particular things, as we do in science and philosophy, but refuse to investigate the cause of all such things?

3. Surely intelligent people today don't believe in God?

Although faith in God does not depend on advanced intellectual abilities, it is a historical fact that many of the greatest and most influential minds in history (including Aristotle, Plato, Augustine, Aquinas, Descartes, Newton, Kant, and many others) not only believed in God but offered various proofs for God's existence. Moreover, believers are to be found among the leading scientists and philosophers today, examples being Francis Collins, John Polkinghorne, and Alasdair MacIntyre. Although it is probably true to say that practical, everyday atheism is increasing in some countries of the Western world today, the causes of this increase are more easily traced to social and ethical changes rather than new intellectual advances or arguments.

4. Isn't the universe full of chaos, disorder and blind chance?

The appearance of chaos, disorder and blind chance in the cosmos can be understood, at least in part, as the spontaneity and rich creativity of a universe that God intended to be more like a garden than a machine. Moreover, spontaneity depends upon underlying order, just as the roll of a dice can generate random numbers, but the dice itself is a carefully constructed and precise object. In the case of the universe, the spontaneity we observe, which assists creativity, also depends on an extraordinary degree of underlying order, such as the stability of the laws of physics, the properties of atoms, the speed of light and so on. Seen from a different perspective, therefore, the universe is extraordinarily and precisely ordered.

5. If the universe is filled with purpose, why can't we see what this purpose is?

We can perceive sufficient order in the universe to be able to do science and philosophy, to trust the rationality of our own minds, and to know that God exists as the cause of this order. Yet it is true that we find it difficult to perceive God's purposes in the universe by unaided human reason alone. One Catholic explanation for this difficulty is that we suffer the effects of sin, which separates us from God and clouds our understanding of God's purposes. Conversely, as we grow in God's grace and understanding of revelation, our perception of creation will also tend to change. Indeed, this perception of nature often becomes more ordered and beautiful with grace, the effects of which can be seen in the great works of Christian art.

6. If God causes everything, what caused God?

The question implies that everything, including God, has to have a cause, but this assertion is not the starting point of any argument about God's existence. The starting point is that all dependent things (atoms, forces, dust, clouds, stars, plants, animals, minds, and so on) do not cause themselves, but must be caused by another. This chain of causation must come to an end with some being that is uncaused, which is what all human beings naturally call 'God'. Without such a principle there could not be anything at all, just as a house needs ultimately to rest on some foundation even if this foundation is invisible. Furthermore, many people who claim to be atheists implicitly accept this argument, since they propose an impersonal substitute for an intelligent Creator rather than rejecting the need for a first cause (or 'God') outright. For example, some now claim that a 'multiverse', beyond direct physical observation, is sufficient to cause the observable universe, although in practice this hypothesis merely pushes back certain problems rather than solving them.

7. Hasn't modern science shown that human beings are simply clever animals?

Modern science has not shown that human beings are simply clever animals, if by 'clever' we mean that all the intellectual abilities of human beings are found in non-human animals in less developed forms. As illustrations of the difference, the philosopher Wittgenstein said that a dog knows its master, but not that its master is coming home the day after tomorrow, and G. K. Chesterton observed (*Everlasting Man*, I.1) that birds build nests, but they do not build nests in the gothic style. Such examples illustrate the general lesson that non-human animals do not think in terms of 'the day after tomorrow' or any other abstract ideas that make language, art, architecture, ethics, science, philosophy or theology possible. Moreover, all non-human animals are satisfied to be what they are, but the human person seeks ultimate happiness and is discontent with finite, created things alone.

8. What if I don't want to be with God, or don't feel any alienation at all?

There are many reasons why we might not want to be with God or simply feel indifferent about him. Even if we believe that there is a God, when we reflect on how he is eternal, all-powerful and all-knowing, we may feel utterly distant and detached from him. Revelation also teaches that sin has separated us from God, causing us to recoil from him and fill our lives with other things. Nevertheless, it is difficult to feel permanently indifferent about God. For example, experiences of extraordinary goodness and beauty, or extraordinary suffering, as well as any sustained reflection on the meaning of life, often awaken the impulse to seek God.

9. There may be a lack of peace in the world, but how can God be the answer when religions are so different from one another and bring so much division?

Religion is commonly recognised as a natural good insofar as it promotes at least some social peace by binding communities together. This social benefit is acknowledged by the possible root of the word 'religion' in *religare*, meaning 'to bind fast' and by the way that civilisations have often built cities around temples. This benefit is even shown by the fact that many atheist states have a history of enthroning dictators as national 'gods', effectively inventing substitutes for religion in order to bind their societies together. These benefits of social cohesion, however, should not obscure the fact that not all particular religions are true and good, and some can even be capricious and cruel. Moreover, even a good and holy religion that promotes true and lasting peace can and should disturb worldly peace and complacency when there is evil to be fought, e.g. the struggle against slavery or abortion. God as revealed through Jesus Christ is a God of love, however, a love that calls us to love even our enemies. This love ultimately brings about a divine peace within the human heart that is more secure and lasting than any social unity imposed by worldly means.

10. Even if the misuse of free will explains some human suffering, why do animals and the natural world suffer if God is good?

There is no wholly agreed answer to this question, but most responses fall into the following groups: (a) there is a curse on creation because of the sins of rational creatures (human beings and angels), as hinted at by *Gn* 3:17, "*Cursed is the ground (earth) because of you;*" or (b) animal suffering is a consequence of God limiting his direct intervention and endowing creation with a 'freedom to wander', leaving open the possibility that evolutionary development will wander at times into 'natural evil'; or (c) animals may experience and react to pain, but do not think about pain, let alone think about thinking about pain, as human beings do when they say, "I am suffering" or "I cannot take any more." Animals are therefore incapable of suffering in the way that conscious human beings do. Some of these responses overlap and yet the truth may turn out to be some other further explanation. What the Catholic faith does teach on this question, however, is that the present world is indeed in a state of suffering and bondage to decay, but also that God has promised *"new heaven and new earth"* for the saints where *"every tear will be wiped away"* (*Rv* 21:4).

11. Some suffering may have a larger and good purpose, but surely a lot of suffering, like bad toothache, is just pointless and unpleasant?

The Catholic faith asks an even more challenging question, namely what is the point of anything at all, even the greatest achievements and pleasures, in the absence of God's offer of eternal life? Without such hope, it is not just suffering but all of life that is ultimately pointless, given that it ends in dust and death. Faith provides a different perspective, however, and while the Christian will suffer apparently random annoyances, difficulties and pain like everyone else, these things cannot, in themselves, extinguish this hope, and they can even be turned to some good for the Christian life. In addition, however strange it may seem except to those advanced in the spiritual life, many of the saints in this life actively seek out deprivation, annoyances and hardship to draw closer to God, and to allow him to soften and 'melt' their hearts to love more purely and deeply. Moreover, they also perceive such sufferings as opportunities to make offerings of themselves, in union with the sacrifice of Christ on the cross, to help bring the grace of salvation to others.

12. Surely we need to be stubborn and look out for ourselves?

Since we are beings made for true friendship with God and others, to be stubborn and to put ourselves first to the exclusion of others is ultimately self-defeating, like the miser who dies rich, alone and miserable. So we need to care for others even if we are simply looking out for our own interests. Christianity invites us to go further, however, and to have hearts that are on fire with divine love, ready to sacrifice even that which we would normally grasp for ourselves in the absence of our relationship with God. Such sacrifices, whether of small and great things, can help to melt our hearts and to increase our capacity for love and happiness. Paradoxically, to look for ourselves in the greatest and noblest sense therefore requires us to be ready to sacrifice ourselves out of love. Jesus himself speaks about this paradox, *"Those who want to save their life will lose it, and those who lose their life for my sake will save it"* (*Lk* 9:24).

13. Isn't the story of Adam and Eve just a pious myth, disproved by modern science?

Rather than a pious myth, the story of Adam and Eve might be better described as a revealed, symbolic history. As a parallel, if one imagines far in the future writing a divinely inspired account of the story of Henry VIII by means of symbols and without any names or other details, one might write the story of a king tempted by a serpent to disobey God and betray his wife because of lust, fear of the future and a desire for power and riches, a decision that leads to great destruction, suffering, upheaval and ultimately to war in his kingdom after his death. The story would then read like a parable, but that does not mean that the story would lack a basis in real events, lost to human records but known to God. Similarly the story of Adam and Eve can sound like a parable of the deadly consequences of sin, and clearly there are elements of the Genesis account that are intended symbolically. Nevertheless, the story also witnesses to some primeval disaster, of a fall of the first human beings from a state of friendship and harmony with God and nature.

14. If Adam and Eve sinned, why do we all have to suffer the consequences?

A world in which sin had no consequences for future generations would be a world without cause and effect, and so alien that it is hard for us even to imagine. Instead, although our histories, societies, and personalities have been shaped by God's goodness, grace and mercy, they have also been shaped by sin and its effects. Moreover, given the status of being the progenitors of the human race, it is not suprising that the choices of the first human persons would have wide ranging spiritual as well as biological effects for their offspring, including ourselves. The good news of Christianity, however, is that we can be saved from sin and its effects and that we can live with the hope of heaven.

15. Do people really thirst for God? Surely many are uninterested.

People clearly thirst for something, in the sense that they seem dissatisfied and unable to be fully and permanently happy with any finite created things. Advertisers exploit this thirst by hinting that people will find true and lasting happiness from the products they are helping to sell, but they offer nothing that can fully satisfy us. Dissatisfaction with other things does not mean that people have an innate, conscious yearning for God, however, since this is the ultimate 'acquired taste', one that grows as one comes to know God and know about God through study and prayer. Nevertheless, Christian revelation and the testimony of the saints affirm that knowing and loving God is also the only way truly to satisfy the restless human heart.

16. Why does God initially choose just one people rather than revealing himself to everyone?

According to revelation, God chose the whole of humanity at its beginning, and desires all people to be saved in the end. For reasons that may remain ultimately mysterious, God chose for us to be offered salvation by means of a saviour. A saviour, however, needed to be born of a woman and born into a particular people who had to be prepared over many centuries for his coming. For this reason, God had to choose one people, and he chose the Jewish people to have this unique role in history.

17. If God was uniquely close to the Jewish people, why did they suffer so much?

There are several reasons why those who come close to God may suffer in various ways. First, most people in this life who draw close to God need to be purified morally and intellectually, a process that is medicinal but also often painful. Second, evil forces in the world can envy and resent those who are chosen and blessed by God, and such forces may single them out for malicious persecution. Third, God may ask those who draw close to him to suffer with him out of love, for the sake of the salvation of others. The history of the Jewish people, who have given the world Jesus Christ, the Catholic Church, all the books of the Bible and remarkable contributions to science, medicine and culture, is evidence of the supernatural fruitfulness of their unique but almost unimaginably costly vocation.

18. Don't experts tell us that much of what is written in the Bible is untrustworthy since it is wrong, of dubious origin, or distorted by people with agendas?

The Bible consists of seventy-three books composed across several centuries and contains many different literary genres, including literal and symbolic histories, poems, metaphors, dreams and parables. So it is not a simple matter to adjudicate on the accuracy of any particular part of the Bible unless one understands the genre and purpose of that part, which is not always apparent. Where the Bible is clearly referring to historical events, there are many known points of correspondence with archaeology and other sources. On many other matters, we lack independent corroboration, yet this lack is not evidence of falsity and the biblical record should be treated fairly as a source in itself. As for the claim of distortion, biblical scholarship over the past two centuries has confirmed the substantial integrity of many of the texts since the early Church. In addition, distortion requires motive, yet the biblical accounts rarely seem to corroborate or lend support to the worldly motives of anyone. Indeed, those who interact with God in the biblical accounts generally endure much pain and sacrifice, the fruits of which are often seen only long afterwards.

19. Don't the people in the Old Testament also do a lot of killing at God's command?

The Old Testament contains numerous prohibitions against unlawful killing, and even accidental murderers were ordered to be exiled (*Nb* 35:25). The only killing in the Old Testament that is permitted, although often still leaving a stain on the perpetrator, is at the behest of legitimate public authority in the context of warfare, capital punishment, and self-defence. In these cases, one or more lives are brought to an end in order to prevent some evil that is serious enough to contaminate or destroy the eternal fruitfulness of others, the nation, or even the whole world. It is from the latter perspective, for example, that the killings involved in the wars to occupy and defend the Promised Land of Canaan should principally be understood, namely obedience to an exceptional divine command to clear the dark and deadly spiritual jungle of paganism and to begin the long centuries of preparation in this particular land for the birth of a saviour. Moreover, these events have a spiritual interpretation that remains valuable today: that the entire dark jungle of vices has to be uprooted in order for the human soul (symbolised by the Promised Land) to flourish as a garden of grace. Yet God may bring even those who died in these historical conflicts to eternal fruitfulness, since revelation teaches that death is not the end of personal existence. The case of an intentional murderer is different, however, since he cuts off another person's life and fruitfulness prematurely and irreparably by claiming for himself the right to destroy another.

Why Christ?

1. Why is Jesus so special? Haven't there been many prophets and messiahs?

Jesus was unlike all other prophets, who customarily spoke words from God and foretold what would happen. Only Jesus claimed and showed, by his words and actions, that he is also divine, the only-begotten Son of the Father, *"I am the way, and the truth, and the life; no one comes to the Father, but by me"* (*Jn* 14:6). Indeed, rather than being simply another prophet, he fulfilled all the prophecies of the Old Testament. Jesus was also unlike all other messiahs who have offered earthly liberation, peace and prosperity. Jesus alone, by contrast, has offered forgiveness of sins, victory over death, and entry to the kingdom of heaven.

2. If Jesus was sent by God, why was he so obscure when he was born?

Jesus was not only sent by God, but he is God, a fact that would make his birth, even into a life of the greatest privilege, riches and honour, unimaginably humble. Nevertheless, he chose relative poverty and obscurity, and whatever the divine motive, his choice teaches us at least two lessons. First, in response to the perverse human tendency to seek God as a means to worldly power and wealth, we need to share God's love and humility if we are to know him and be one with him. Second, the fact that Jesus is now acknowledged in many ways as the pivotal figure of history, teaches us also that God's power to transform the world is unlike worldly power and does not in any way depend on natural resources and honour.

3. Does the Bible actually say that Jesus is God and that he claimed to be God?

Yes, the Bible says explicitly that Jesus is God. An example of such a statement is when St Thomas says to the risen Jesus, *"My Lord and my God"* (*Jn* 20:28). Jesus has the 'fullness of God' (*Col* 1:19), and often refers to himself as the 'Son' or the 'beloved Son', who is 'one' with his heavenly Father (*Jn* 10:30). Scripture also describes occasions when Jesus is worshipped (cf. *Mt* 2:1; *Mt* 14:33; *Jn* 9:38) and affirms his power not only to work miracles but to forgive sins (cf. *Mk* 2:1-12), an ability attributed uniquely to God by those listening. The Bible also records instances when Jesus confirmed his divinity in response to statements or questions asked by others. When asked the following question directly by the high priest, *"Are you the Christ, the Son of the Blessed?"* Jesus responded, *"I am"* (*Mk* 14:61-62; cf. *Mt* 26:63-64). Furthermore, the fact that Jesus was then condemned to death for blasphemy shows that his listeners had understood clearly his claim to be divine.

4. Jesus may have worked miracles two thousand years ago, but why can't we see spectacular signs of his power today?

Jesus taught that it is more blessed to believe without seeing and miracles, at best, remove obstacles to faith rather than implanting genuine faith or nurturing the love of God. Nevertheless, the Gospels and other early Christian texts underline how miracles can sometimes play an important role in the life of faith, and that there was a unique intensity of miracles at the beginning of the Church to confirm the proclamation of the faith at its inception. Since that time, miracles have tended to be exceptional, normally to remind the Church of important supernatural truths or to promote some change or new venture, such as the miracles attributed to St Augustine of Canterbury when he was sent by Pope Gregory to convert the Anglo-Saxons. Nevertheless, we can see the effects of many spectacular signs of Jesus' power at work today, examples being the instantaneous cures associated with holy shrines and the recognition of saints, evidence for which has to be subjected to scientific and medical tests. Other miracles in recent times include the 'Miracle of the Sun' at Fatima, seen by seventy thousand people, the Eucharistic hosts at Siena that have not decayed for around three centuries, and the bodies of certain saints, such as Bernadette, that have been miraculously preserved from the normal processes of decay. Finally, the Church herself can be regarded as a spectacular sign of Jesus' power, especially for those who study history deeply, since she is arguably the only organisation that has survived for two thousand years while perpetually facing threats, defeat and annihilation.

5. What is a 'sin', and why would I need anyone else to forgive my sins?

A sin is a deliberate evil action: a thought, word, deed or omission contrary to God's will. By opposing our will to God's will, we also either damage (in the case of 'venial sin') or betray (in the case of 'mortal sin') our union of grace with God, which separates and partly isolates us from God. This loss of God also introduces disorder into our relationships with others and disharmony into ourselves. Although laws, a disciplined life, and a combination of rewards and punishments may help to mitigate some of the most overtly destructive effects of this loss, there is no satisfactory and complete human solution. For this reason, we need God's help and, more specifically, God's forgiveness of our sins and restoration of the grace of baptism (usually by the Sacrament of Confession) to restore our union with him and to begin to re-order our lives.

6. How do we know these texts have not been corrupted or altered for propaganda?

Intensive scholarship over the last two centuries has confirmed the substantial integrity of the New Testament texts. This finding is further supported by the continuity of manuscripts, with minor textual variations, going back as far back as we have evidence. Moreover, the vast number and variety of scriptural references in the works of authors throughout the first few Christian centuries reveals that they had access to substantially the same sacred texts as we do today. For these reasons we have confidence that there has been no significant corruption or alteration of these texts.

7. How can a person be a message, or a 'word' (of God or anything else)?

One reason why Jesus is both personal and called the 'Word of God' (*Jn* 1:1) is because he reveals God perfectly. All other words for God are partial or imperfect, such as metaphors ("*God is a consuming fire*" [*Heb* 12:19]) or analogies ("*God is living*" [*1 Th* 1:9]) or descriptions of God's action ("*God made heaven and earth*" [*Gn* 1:1]). By contrast, Jesus Christ is the perfect Word of God because he is God, the only-begotten Son of the Father. So Jesus Christ, as true God and true man, is like a bridge between humanity and God, between earth and heaven. The coming of the person of Jesus Christ is therefore also the coming of the true Word of God and a message of good news for humanity.

8. If Jesus is God, and his Father is God, and the Spirit is God, are there three gods?

To be personal is to be relational, and to love involves relationship. So the Christian teaching that God is personal and that God is love is consistent and harmonious with God being a Trinity of lover, beloved and the love that is between them. Moreover, this principle of a unity that maintains personal distinctions has inspired the kind of good developments in society that are commonly associated with true revelation, such as the institution of Christian marriage, the notion of Christian friendship, and the vision of society in which distinct institutions work in mutual harmony. Conversely, religions that have no imprint or foreshadowing of the Trinity, or explicitly deny the Trinity, have a tendency to regard what they worship as impersonal, inscrutable and even unloving and capricious, an understanding of the divine that is often reflected in the kinds of societies that they produce. Yet Christ's revelation that God is Father, Son and Holy Spirit does not mean that there are three gods, since what is a unity in one sense can be trinitarian in another. For example, the three sides of a triangle are three insofar as they are sides, but are inseparably one insofar as they are a triangle. So although the Trinity undoubtedly exceeds human comprehension, the teaching about the Trinity that has been drawn from revelation, namely that God is 'one substance, three persons', is not contradictory.

9. Is it not beneficial to draw from all kinds of spiritual traditions?

The term 'spiritual' can encompass the highest goods, such as the life of God and of the saints, but also the most extreme evil, such as witchcraft and the diabolic. What is 'spiritual', in its broadest sense, can therefore turn the human soul or a society into a beautiful sunlit garden for the Lord God, or into a disordered and dark jungle, an abode of spiritual parasites. When drawing from any tradition, careful discrimination is therefore needed to distinguish between good and evil. So when the Church draws from and infuses elements of diverse cultural traditions, as she often does, the faithful are helped to sift good from evil under the inspiration of the Holy Spirit, and then they gradually transfigure the good elements to make them holy.

10. If God can do anything, why was Christ needed to end our separation from God?

Our separation from God is not physical but involves the breaking of a personal relationship of love with God and a consequent coldness and stubbornness of our wills. God cannot rescue us by overriding our wills, however, without us making us like automatons that are incapable of love, just as God cannot do anything else that implies contradiction, such as changing the past or making a square circle. Being unable to reach up to God, metaphorically speaking, it is therefore fitting that God would end our separation by reaching down to us, becoming a man like us. Whether God could have chosen another way to save us is impossible to answer, although the anguished prayer of Jesus in Gethsemane implies that the sacrifice of Christ, the Incarnate Son of God was required (*Mt* 26:39). What should be clear, however, is that the way God has chosen is fitting and a supreme confirmation of his love for us.

11. How can a cruel death of an innocent man, let alone of God himself, take sin away rather than curse the world still more?

Scripture and Tradition are clear that Jesus' sacrificial death has ransomed us from sin and reconciled us to God, whether or not we understand how this atonement has been carried out. As St Peter says, *"You know that you were ransomed...with the precious blood of Christ"* (*1 P* 1:18). Scripture also assures us of the many fruits of Christ's sacrifice. By means of his sacrifice, Jesus has: repaid our debt of guilt (*Mt* 20:28); gained mercy for us and repealed our punishment (*Mt* 26:28); defeated the claims of the devil over us (*Jn* 12:31); reconciled us to God (*2 Co* 5:19); and fulfilled Scripture and salvation history (*Col* 1:20). On the cross, Jesus therefore suffered the effects of sin for us, his divine love revoking the offence of all sins and bearing the pain and cost of sin in itself. While we do not fully understand how this suffering has healed us, some indication may be seen in the verse, *"He himself bore our sins in his body on the tree, that we might die to sin and live to righteousness. By his wounds you have been healed"* (*1 P* 2:24). In other words, just as in communion we draw life from him, he drew sin and death from us when he was united with us out of love, and it was these things that were hammered out and killed with Christ on the cross.

12. How can a cross, an instrument of torture and death, bring anyone to life or heaven?

Christ's sacrificial death offers us healing from sin and its effects, and so the cross is venerated as the instrument of this victory, not for its cruelty but as a symbol of the love of the Son of God that led him to lay down his life to save us from sin, death and hell. Moreover, the cross also serves as a sobering reminder of the need to put to death whatever is in us that is at war with God, and of the opportunity that is ours to offer sacrifices in union with Christ's sacrifice, for the sake of the salvation of the world. Finally, because of the resurrection, the cross is also a sign that death has been conquered, so that the cross has become the most important comfort and symbol of hope for all those who have died.

13. If following Christ means suffering and rejection, why is the gospel 'good news' of happiness and joy?

The gospel does not promise ease in this life, but only that a road, which is often hard and narrow, has been opened by Christ leading to eternal happiness. This opening is good news, and the saints, who have followed Christ faithfully along this road, also testify to the further good news that this road brings rest to the soul and a joyful anticipation of the life of heaven, where, *"Every tear will be wiped away"* (*Rv* 21:4).

14. How is it that many people manage to live well and cope with challenges without Christ?

Many people cope with life on an everyday basis seemingly without Christ, but insoluble difficulties remain about the broader purpose of life and final hope of happiness. For example, there is always the risk of losing those things that people usually rely on to live well, such as health, wealth and relationships. Moreover, people may also wonder, and be unable to answer, the question of whether life has any point, since we die soon and our achievements usually fade and die soon afterwards. In addition, although people may value love, they may also find themselves unable to find love or joy, signs of which can be seen in the epidemics of drug abuse, self-destructiveness, narcissism and nihilism in contemporary life. Christ, by his conquest of sin and death, his offer of divine love, and invitation to follow him to the kingdom of heaven, is alone is able to resolve these problems, *"I have come that they may have life, and have it abundantly"* (*Jn* 10:10).

15. Why do we still have to die if Christ has conquered death?

Prior to Christ's victory, death was something to be feared, bringing our limited mortal life to an end and opening the prospect of punishment for sin and separation from God for eternity. By his resurrection, Christ has not taken away our physical death. Indeed, without such death, we would be left to endure unending years in a decaying and corrupting world, an immortality that would not be a blessing but ultimately a curse. Instead, he has transformed death, so that as we follow him into eternity in union with him, our death is transformed into a blessing, opening the prospect of the resurrection and everlasting happiness.

16. If Christ had the power to rise from the dead, why was he left still wounded?

This question has a variety of answers. First, the wounds show, as nothing else can, that the Jesus who was crucified is the same Jesus who was raised and stands before his disciples, not some imposter or anti-Christ. Second, the wounds are a sign of the supernatural changes to Jesus' resurrected body, since they are no longer defects, as they would be in this present life, but are now marks of his triumph. Third, since we are called to follow Christ, they are a sign that any wounds sustained in this world for the sake of salvation become part of what we are in eternity, and that these wounds contribute to our glory.

17. Why did Jesus Christ only appear to those who had known and followed him before his death, and why did many of them also fail to recognise him?

Jesus' resurrected body is physical, but the changes to his body and its powers also signify that he is the first fruit of a new, immortal and sinless creation, which nothing from this old creation will be able to see or enter without the salvation he offers. So it is fitting that the risen Jesus is only seen by those who seek this salvation by faith, and who are already on the threshold of this new kingdom of God. Indeed, the fact that they have some difficulty recognising him at first may be in part due to the changes to his body and powers. Nevertheless, although Jesus only appeared to certain witnesses, their number and variety gives a secure foundation for belief on the basis of testimonial evidence. Indeed, St Paul records that the risen Jesus had appeared to several hundred people (*1 Co* 15:6). There is not one instance of any of these witnesses denying the resurrection later, even in the face of persecution and death, and those who opposed the gospel could not offer any evidence of Jesus' dead body, since the tomb in which Jesus had been laid after his crucifixion was found to be empty on the third day, despite being under a Roman guard (*Mt* 27:66). Finally, certain physical signs in the world today may bear witness, indirectly, to the truth of the resurrection of Jesus Christ. In particular, the bodies of some of the saints, such as St Bernadette, have not decayed in the normal way and remain in good condition for decades or even centuries (cf. *Ac* 2:27). While the souls of these saints are in heaven, the preservation of their bodies from normal decay may be interpreted as a foreshadowing or prophecy of the final resurrection from the dead at the end of time.

18. In many of these encounters Jesus suddenly appears or vanishes; doesn't that suggest that he was a ghostly projection?

The accounts of Jesus after his resurrection describe him showing the wounds of his crucifixion to his disciples, inviting them to touch him, and eating and drinking with them, actions that would be impossible for a ghost or disembodied soul made visible. The message of the Gospels is therefore that Jesus was raised body and soul from death and blessed with powers appropriate for the new and immortal life of glory.

19. Even if many followers of Jesus died for their faith, isn't that commitment found in many other kinds of religions, beliefs and cults?

A commitment of fidelity to death is not unique, although the Christian commitment is unusual in its frequency and scale throughout history, especially during the terrible persecutions of the twentieth century. What characterises genuine Christian commitment, however, is that fidelity to the point of dying is done from a motive of supernatural love, not hate, and certainly not a desire to immolate oneself to destroy others. One sign of this motive is the fact that those recognised Christian saints who have been put to death for their faith are often on record as forgiving their enemies, and praying that their persecutors be reconciled to God.

Why the Church?

1. Isn't organised religion, including the Church, the source of much evil and best avoided?

All varieties of religion, whether organised or not, can be sources of evil or misused by evil people, but there are several ways in which organised religion is morally superior to mere transient associations of individual believers. First, many achievements, whether in the natural world or in human societies, are only possible with a high degree of organisation, continuity through time, and specialisation of roles. Similarly, it is the organised unity of the Catholic faith over time that shaped the foundations of a unified and ethical Western legal tradition and made possible contributions to many other fields including art, architecture, music, literature, languages, and exploration. Second, only an organised religion can act with authority to disown or stop people doing evil in its name. Third, organisation and order are inherently good states in contrast to chaos and disorder. Finally, it should be noted that organisation and order are not and do not need to be stifling or restrictive, and that the Catholic Church is organised more like a garden than a machine.

2. Didn't the Catholic Church appear long after the time of Jesus Christ, an invention of later men of power like the Emperor Constantine?

No, the term 'Catholic Church' is first mentioned in a letter written around AD 107 by a bishop, St Ignatius of Antioch, who wrote "*Wherever Jesus Christ is, there is the Catholic Church*" (*Epistle to the Smyrnaeans*, 8), over two centuries before Constantine became emperor. Moreover, records from the first three centuries describe a Church that is recognisably 'Catholic': for example, the ministries of bishop, priest and deacon; Holy Communion treated as the body and blood of Jesus Christ; a special honour accorded to Mary as the 'Second Eve' and 'Mother of God', and the recognised importance of union with the See of Rome, the final place of the ministries of the apostles Ss Peter and Paul. So although the Catholic Church today has evolved and developed over history, she is also in organic continuity with the Church of the apostles of Jesus Christ.

3. Why do we need the Pope and the other bishops if we have the Bible and faith in Jesus Christ?

Although the Bible is the entire content of God's inspired written truth, it does not follow that the Bible alone can teach us everything we need to know about revelation. First, the Bible is a difficult book requiring careful interpretation, especially as many truths are expressed as parables or signs. Second, even an infallible text, interpreted by imperfect individuals, can be used to justify all kinds of evil. Third, the Protestant movement, initiated by Martin Luther in 1517, which claimed to rely on the Bible alone and on faith in Jesus without the Catholic Church, has since fragmented into between 8,000 and 30,000 different groups. As the early Christians realised when faced with various doctrinal controversies, it is necessary to appeal to the oral tradition passed down from the apostles and to have a final, infallible authority to adjudicate among interpretations of Scripture. Furthermore, early Christians realised that God has blessed us with such an authority in the teaching office of the Church. While Scripture does not support the Protestant claim that Scripture alone is sufficient, it does tell us that the Church is "*the pillar and bulwark of the truth*" (*1 Tm* 3:15).

4. The Church may claim to have authority, but what makes this claim at all credible?

If God loves us and desires us to know the truth about him and how we should live, he needs to provide us with an authoritative and reliable teacher so that our faith has a firm foundation. Across the vast range of communities described as 'Christian' in the world today, the only candidate for this teaching and governing role that is still in organic continuity with the Church of the apostles is the teaching office of the Catholic Church, exercised by the Pope, the successor of St Peter, and those bishops in communion with him.

5. The birth and early growth of the Church narrated here seems rapid and full of wonder. Why does Christianity seem to be in decline in some places today?

The Catholic Church has about a billion members today, which is not exactly a sign of failure although levels of commitment vary and there is decline in some countries. The paradox of the Catholic Church through the centuries, however, is that she has been threatened and on the edge of annihilation through every century of her existence. For example, the Roman historian Tacitus, in his *Annals of the Roman*

Republic, describes early Christians being burned alive in Nero's pleasure gardens (15.44), which was not a promising beginning for the Roman Church. Nevertheless, the Catholic Church eventually proved to be the unique organised entity to survive from the Roman Empire. There may be a divine reason for this paradox of strength and weakness, insofar as God may intervene to avoid the Church appearing too successful in worldly terms, in case people are tempted to join and manipulate her from evil motives. Yet the wonderful truth is that the Church, like Christ, always rises from the dead, just when she seems dead and buried to the world.

6. Aren't there many good Christians who are not Catholic?

St Cyprian, a bishop and martyr in the third century, wrote, *"He cannot have God for his father, who has not the Church for his mother"* (*Treatise on Unity*, 6), emphasising the importance of all Christians being members of the Church. The condition of being separated from the Church is only sinful when one is cut off from the Church due to one's own fault. Nevertheless, such a state is always unsatisfactory because the Church is deprived of full communion with one of her members and that person is deprived of the spiritual blessings and most of the sacraments of the Church. So although it is possible to be good in certain ways while not being in communion with the Catholic Church, this is not the full measure of goodness intended by Jesus Christ, who founded one Church on the rock of the apostle Peter (*Mt* 16:18; cf. 18:17).

7. Hasn't the Church held people back, intellectually and morally?

The Church that provided the faith of Europe at the birth of the Western legal system and university system, the faith of St Augustine of Hippo, St Francis of Assisi, St Thomas Aquinas, Michelangelo, Leonardo da Vinci, St Hildegard of Bingen and St Teresa of Ávila, and whose priests invented the Big Bang theory and genetics, cannot be lightly dismissed as holding people back intellectually, morally or by any other standard of human flourishing. For more examples of the fruits of the Catholic faith, see also pages 38-41.

8. If the Church aims to produce saints in heaven, why is it full of sinners?

Just as a medical hospital aims at restoring health, and hence is always full of sick people, the Church is a spiritual hospital that is always full of sinners, hopefully who also want to become saints. This sinfulness is a consequence of free will and a spirit of rebellion against God, which persists even after baptism and against which any Christian will need to engage in spiritual warfare, principally by means of prayer, fasting, and giving to those in need. The essential goodness and holiness of the Church is shown, however, in the fact that at least some of her children have definitely become great saints in heaven.

9. Why do we need complex things like sacraments and rules? Isn't it enough to have faith in Jesus?

Scripture never tells us that faith alone is enough for salvation, but presents a rich diversity of interconnected gifts, dispositions and fruits, including: grace (*Ep* 2:5); hope (*Rm* 8:24); divine love (*1 Co* 2:9); baptism (*Mk* 16:16); membership of the Church or 'body of Christ' (*1 Co* 12:12-13); the body and blood of Christ (*Jn* 6:54); keeping God's commandments (*Mt* 19:17); and fruitfulness in good works (*Mt* 7:19). Catholics interpret these and other characteristics of salvation mentioned in Scripture as various facets and stages of the life of the grace that normally begins with baptism. Even without any details about how these elements fit together, it should be apparent that salvation is a process that lasts a lifetime, a parallel for which can be seen in the way that a plant grows towards the harvest. To support and protect this supernatural fruitfulness, it is a blessing, not a burden, that God should make available a rich diversity of sacraments and rules for safeguarding this growth from the poison of sin.

10. Hasn't the Church been the source of much evil as well as good in the world?

The straightforward answer is 'yes', because Catholics living in the world are generally sinners, like all human beings, and as such often betray their own faith and cause evil in the world. Furthermore, Catholics would add that the sins of believers, who have knowledge of the gospel and of good Christian practice, are often more culpable than the sins of unbelievers. Nevertheless, to claim that the Church herself, in regard to her properly understood structure and teaching, is a cause of evil is a much more difficult case to make for three reasons. First, the Church traces her origins to Christ, who was without sin. Second, any case against the Church presupposes that one can first agree some objective standard of ultimate good and evil without reference to God and faith, yet there is little agreement on how such a standard can be recognised and be broadly accepted. Third, we do know that the Church, throughout each and every century of her existence, has communicated the divine gifts required for at least some human beings to become saints when they are truly faithful to her teaching. This fruitfulness from lives of extreme holiness suggests that the Church herself is good and holy, and it is only the infidelity of many of her members that causes evil.

11. How can the Church take credit for human achievements that might have been accomplished anyway, or even better, without faith?

The Church rarely takes credit directly for any specific human achievement, given that many causes are invariably at work. Nevertheless, it is a fact of history that many widely acknowledged achievements of civilisation, such as the Western university and legal systems, Western art, musical notation, gothic architecture, hospitals, nursing care and much else were initially the fruits of Catholic societies. Moreover, rather than being accidental developments, a plausible account of at least some causal connections between the faith and these achievements can be given in many of these cases. For example, the university is a type of 'corporate person', legally speaking, a natural extension of the Catholic philosophy of the person in the Middle Ages; Western art is representational and not merely abstract, because of the Catholic belief that art can and should represent what is associated with the Incarnation, the Word made flesh. Musical notation was a fruit of monastic singing in worship; Christian architecture evolved to be beautiful for the liturgical and sacramental life of the Church; hospitals were mandated by the First Ecumenical Council of the Church in 325; and nursing care first developed from the work of the religious orders in caring for the sick and dying, in obedience to Christian teaching about the importance of the works of mercy. The principles that first inspired these developments are so closely associated with the Christian faith that it is hard to see how they would have developed, at least in the form they did, in the absence of such faith.

12. Hasn't the Church (and Western civilisation in general) damaged and ruined other cultures, as well as the environment?

The Church aims to incorporate and transfigure rather than obliterate other cultures, with the exception of those practices that are clearly and irredeemably evil. For example, the faith brought the bloody human sacrifices of the Aztec Empire to an end, but the image of Our Lady of Guadalupe, a remarkable icon of the mother of Jesus Christ and hence of the Mother of God, incorporates Aztec symbolism into an image of immaculate holiness. As another example, the work of Catholic architects like Augustus Pugin helped to instil divine beauty into the soulless cityscapes of Britain during the industrial revolution. To give yet another example, Catholic missionaries continue to develop written forms of some of the more obscure languages of the world, providing many societies with their first written records and preserving knowledge that might otherwise be lost. With regard to the environment, those lands that have been under the stewardship of societies deeply infused with the Catholic faith for many centuries, such as central Italy and ancient monastic lands, often witness to an ordered way of life in harmony with nature. More recent Western societies, by contrast, often lack this harmony and engender some environmental damage, but many of the proximate origins of these societies can be traced to more materialistic and pragmatic philosophies than Catholicism.

13. Aren't many of the saints rather peculiar and extreme?

The recognised saints have gone much further in allowing God to transform their lives than is usual even for faithful Christians, so it is not surprising that their lives sometimes seem extreme from a mundane, worldly perspective. Nevertheless, even if we cannot fully understand the saints as they understand themselves in the light of God, what we do generally see in the world is the immense fruitfulness of the saints, especially in terms of the blessings and transformations of the lives of those who are influenced by them.

14. Can't I live a good life without going to church?

You would be deeply grieved if you were a parent whose child never does anything wrong but who also never speaks with you or listens to you, and who behaves as if you are not even there. Indeed, you would probably prefer a situation in which your child sometimes does wrong, but also comes back and speaks to you, repents of what he or she has done wrong, and works to repair the damage done. Similarly with our own lives, God's purpose in making us was so that we could know him and love him. For this reason, God wants us to pray and to be in communion with the Church which is his family in the life of grace. So no life that is cut off from the life of the Church can ever be wholly good in God's eyes.

15. Why does God want or need to send us out on mission, if he is all-powerful?

Human beings have free will, and the ultimate source of all the most serious human problems is the misuse of this freedom to do evil. God cannot solve these problems by overriding our wills, for such an action would suspend our freedom and turn us into robots. So God comes to our hearts initially as a stranger standing and knocking at the door, *"If anyone hears my voice and opens the door, I will come in to him and will dine with him, and he with me"* (Rv 3:20). In other words, since we have free will, only we can open the door and allow Christ to enter our lives, leading us to true freedom in communion with him. Such an appeal, to open the door of our hearts, is usually best made person-to-person. This is one way to understand why God came to us in the flesh in Jesus Christ, and why he in turn sends us out to proclaim his message to others.

16. If we focus on heaven, doesn't that mean we neglect this world?

The Christian writer C.S. Lewis said that in this life we write the title page of what we are to be in eternity. From this perspective, far from neglecting this world, we regard our lives here as infinitely precious and important, and not some temporary testing ground or obstacle on the way to heaven. Moreover, history teaches that those with deep Christian faith and love have not neglected to invest time in works of great and lasting value to civilisation on earth, such as: founding universities, hospitals and schools; advancing science; painting; composing music; developing languages; writing literature; and so on. In particular, the lives of the recognised saints have brought great blessings to earth as well as to heaven. So a focus on heaven is often a source of widely acknowledged blessing rather than neglect of this world.

17. Isn't everyone a child of God, not just saints or Christians generally?

To become a child of God through Baptism is one of the unique gifts of Christianity, which is why it is so unusual to call God "Our Father" outside of Christianity. God desires, of course, that all people become his adopted children, but the grace that makes this relationship possible is not an innate disposition of human nature, but has to be received as a gift from God, usually by means of the Sacrament of Baptism.

18. Surely a lot of the Church's rules, especially in sexual matters, are out-of-date, bigoted or unequal?

Many of the Church's rules in sexual matters merely express, clarify and support what is written into our natures, namely that as biological beings, male and female, we procreate sexually and that a husband and wife should fully commit to one another in marriage to care for the children they may conceive together. Moreover, as we are also called to a relationship to God that is a covenant, not merely a contract, a specifically Christian marriage takes on some of the characteristics of this divine covenant, especially love and mutual sacrifice. Sexual practices outside this context are either irresponsible or pointless, and they easily degenerate into the mere use of another human being for pleasure. The Church cannot, therefore, regard such practices as 'equal' in value to the sexual union of husband and wife. Moreover, although it is true that modern society has largely rejected this Christian understanding, the visible consequences of the sexual revolution to date include the widespread misery and loneliness of modern society, abortion on an industrial scale, the spread of serious diseases and family breakdown. The crucial question is not, therefore, whether the Church's rules are 'out of date', but whether they are right and good.

19. Why does God want us to pray if he knows what we need already?

God knows that what we most need, whether we are aware of this or not, is to know and love him. God also knows that prayer, by which we speak and listen to God with a desire to be with God and to do his will, helps us to know and love him. So God wants us to pray and will reward prayer, not because he needs information from us, but because praying nourishes us spiritually and helps us to find true happiness with him.

20. What about all the Christians who are not members of the Church?

The Catholic Church recognises all that is good and true in other Christian communions such as, for instance, the validity of the sacraments of the Orthodox churches. Nevertheless, she also holds that Jesus Christ founded only one, visible Church in this world, to which he desires that all Christians belong. The difference between being outside and being in full communion with this Church has been described by one former evangelical minister, who was received into the Catholic Church, as like leaving a raft to board an ocean liner. Christ has equipped this liner with everything necessary to transmit the faith to all generations until the end of the world, and to carry a soul in safety through the storms of life to the shores of heaven.

21. If the Church's message is simple, why are its liturgies, doctrines, laws and practices so very complicated?

The apparent complexity of the Church's life has two sources. First, the gospel possesses inexhaustible spiritual riches. Hence, just as white light seems simple but generates a rich spectrum of beautiful colours when it impacts on certain objects, the Church's communication of God's grace generates rich and detailed liturgical forms, artistic expressions and doctrine. Second, human sin weaves a tangled web, due to the many and complex ways in which people deviate from God. Just as a key needs to be an intricately shaped object to open the door of a prison, so also the Church's laws and practices often need to be intricate to warn people and to help rescue them from the complex and tangled web of sin.

22. Surely it is arrogant to claim that the Church brought light to humanity. Wasn't the Enlightenment, which made the modern world, opposed by the Christian faith?

The Enlightenment was a cultural movement of intellectuals in the seventeenth and eighteenth centuries whose self-proclaimed mission was to transform society through reason, a movement that did indeed shape the modern world. Many Catholics, especially the Jesuits, made important contributions to reason, education and science during this period, but insofar as the Church did come into conflict with aspects of what is called the Enlightenment, it is important to understand that, from a Catholic standpoint, even the name of this movement is deceptive. First, 'enlightenment' suggests that society was in darkness prior to the work of these thinkers. Yet Catholic societies and scholars had already been 'enlightening' the world in dramatic ways since at least the building of Chartres Cathedral and the first genuine universities in the twelfth and thirteenth centuries, followed by the Renaissance from the fourteenth century. Second, close examination of history often reveals that many developments in reason and science credited to the Enlightenment are rooted in breakthroughs made centuries earlier. Third, the kind of reason advanced by many Enlightenment intellectuals was often allied with an aggressive anti-Catholic cultural program, which, from a Catholic perspective, risked obscuring or cutting off the true light of the world, Jesus Christ. Finally, movements associated with the Enlightenment often had dark and malevolent aspects. For example, following the French Revolution in 1793, a 'Goddess of Reason' was placed on the high altar of Notre Dame in Paris, symbolising the new 'Age of Reason'. The very same year, however, the 'Reign of Terror' began, during which tens of thousands were guillotined or otherwise executed, including many Catholic martyrs. These horrors illustrate the truth of Jesus' caution against the deceptions of what can appear good and reasonable at first, but is in reality a mask for evil, "*You will know them by their fruits*" (*Mt* 7:20).

Glossary

Abraham, the ancestral father of the Jewish people (*Gn* 11:26–25:10), left his homeland (c. 2000 BC) in obedience to God, who promised him a new land and numerous descendants. He was the father of Isaac and grandfather of Jacob, also called Israel, and is known as the 'father of faith' for his fidelity (ccc. 59-65, 762, 45-147; *Compendium* 8, 79, 360, 536).

Angels are spiritual beings with intellect and will who were created by God to love and serve him. Those angels who rebelled against God and turned to evil at their creation became 'demons' or 'devils'; their leader is Satan, also called Lucifer or the Devil (ccc. 328-352, 391-395; *Compendium* 74-75, 108).

Apostles, meaning literally 'those who are sent', are the twelve men chosen directly by Jesus Christ to be the leaders and foundations of the 'new Israel', the Church (ccc. 858-860, 857, 860, 981; *Compendium* 12, 15, 109, 174, 175, 180, 273).

Baptism, the sacrament by which we become Christians, frees us from original sin, makes us children of God and members of the Church. The Sacrament of Baptism is conferred by immersion in water or by pouring water over a person's head, together with the words, "[The person's name], I baptise you in the name of the Father, and of the Son, and of the Holy Spirit" (ccc. 1213-1284; *Compendium* 252-264).

Bible, also called 'Sacred Scripture', is a unified collection of seventy-three books: (1) an 'Old Testament' of forty-six books written c. 1200–c. 100 BC, describing creation, the fall and God's subsequent revelations and dealings with the Jewish people; (2) a 'New Testament' of twenty-seven books written c. AD 50–c. 100, with four narratives of the life of Jesus Christ (the Gospels of Matthew, Mark, Luke and John) and other writings (mainly letters by St Paul) about Christ, his message, the early Church, instructions for Christian living and prophecies of the end of the world (ccc. 101-141; *Compendium* 13-24).

Bishops are the successors of the apostles of Jesus Christ, who in turn ordain men to succeed them and hence preserve the continuity of the apostolic office through history. Bishops usually lead the Church in a particular area called a diocese. They are ordained to teach, govern and sanctify the Church in communion with the Pope, the bishop of Rome (ccc. 1555-1561, 880-896; *Compendium* 179-187, 324-327).

Catholic, which means 'universal', is a term properly given to the Church, since she has a mission to the whole world, is present throughout the whole of Christian history, and protects and communicates the entire content of God's revealed truth for salvation (ccc. 830-856; *Compendium* 166-168).

Christ is from a Greek word meaning 'the anointed one' ('Messiah' in Hebrew), the title of a priest, prophet or king in the Old Testament, and especially of a future redeemer ('*the* Christ'). The title is closely associated with Jesus, to the extent that 'Jesus Christ' has become the proper name by which he is known (ccc. 711-716; *Compendium* 8, 78, 82, 111).

Christian denotes any human person who has received the grace of baptism, and who is thereby called by God to live as a disciple of Jesus Christ in his Church (ccc. 915, 1213; *Compendium* 82, 163-168).

Church, the visible body of believers established by Christ on earth to gather all people to divine life in heaven, and which also includes those who have died in God's grace. Her four principal characteristics are that she is one, holy, catholic and apostolic (ccc. 748-945; *Compendium* 147-193). *See also* pages 34-47.

Confession (also called 'penance' or 'reconciliation') is the sacrament by which we, repenting and confessing our sins, are absolved of sin through the ministry of a priest (ccc. 1422-1498; *Compendium* 296-311).

Creation is the act by which God makes, out of nothing, all else that exists. What is created encompasses beings that exist immediately from God's act as well as the complete potential for all other beings to be generated as the universe unfolds ('evolves'). The word also denotes the whole universe that results from God's creative act (ccc. 279-324; *Compendium* 51-54).

David (c. 1040-970 BC) was the second king of Israel, honoured subsequently as a pattern of kingly righteousness. Jesus Christ is the 'Son of David' and king of the 'new Israel', the Church (ccc. 2578-2580; *Compendium* 8).

Death is the cessation of our earthly lives when our souls are separated from our bodies and we cease to choose between good and evil. God's judgement follows death (ccc. 1021-1037; *Compendium* 205-206). *See also* Heaven and hell.

Disciples are students of a master or teacher, from whom they learn not just facts but a whole way of life by close personal association, observation, and imitation. The vocation of every Christian is to be a disciple of Jesus Christ (ccc. 425, 542, 787; *Compendium* 127-129).

Eucharist refers to (1) a sacrifice, also called the Mass, that makes present Jesus Christ's sacrifice on Calvary for our salvation; (2) the real presence of God, being Christ himself under the appearances of bread and wine (a change called 'transubstantiation'); (3) this same heavenly food, also called 'Holy Communion', which we consume to share in God's own life (ccc. 1322-1419; *Compendium* 271-294).

Evangelism means the communication of the Christian faith or 'good news' to others (ccc. 425-429, 905; *Compendium* 80, 172, 190).

Evil. *See* Good and evil.

Faith, the disposition to recognise and acknowledge Christian revelation, is the root of the life of grace (ccc. 142-184; *Compendium* 25-37, 386).

Father, God the. *See* Trinity.

Free will is generally understood as our ability to do different (specifically human) actions than the ones we in fact do, all other influences on us being equal (ccc. 1730-1748; *Compendium* 363-369).

God. *See* pages 6-19 (ccc. 39-41, 199-231; *Compendium* 1-10, 36-43).

God, knowing. *See* Grace.

Good and evil most generally refer to 'that which all things seek', and 'that which all things avoid' respectively. Natural beings such as plants and animals seek to fulfil their own natures automatically, a flourishing that defines what 'good' and 'evil' means to them. Rational beings, however, can choose their goals and can reject or mistake their true good, namely flourishing and happiness with God, instead choosing some evil that seems good to them (ccc. 309-314; *Compendium* 57-58, 368).

Gospels, the four. *See* Bible.

Grace refers to those gifts that bring about a supernatural friendship of a person with God. By our natural abilities we can know that there is a God, but only by grace can we know and love God by sharing God's divine life and becoming his adopted children. Since grace transforms the virtues of human nature, the life of a saint is radically different from a conventionally virtuous life (ccc. 1810-1832, 1996-2005; *Compendium* 362, 420, 423, 424, 425).

Heaven and hell are the two final states of all human and angelic beings. Heaven is our divinely intended eternal home where human nature, transformed by God's grace, attains final and complete love, joy and peace with the vision of God's face. Scripture describes heaven as a city or kingdom where the saints enjoy a new and perfect creation, and the reward they deserve for what they have merited in loving union with God in this life. Those who die in God's grace either go straight to heaven or first enter purgatory, a temporary place of purification for sins and for reparation (ccc. 1023-1029; *Compendium* 209). Just as the life of the saints establishes the pattern or title page of their eternal happiness, so also the prideful choice of evil and a lack of repentance before the end of earthly life establishes a pattern of damnation, a state in which a person rejects God's love permanently and enters hell, the place of punishment of damned souls, the devil and his angels. Christ's sacrifice on Calvary shows that God will do anything to save us from hell, except to take away our freedom to reject him (ccc. 1033-1037; *Compendium* 212-213).

Holy Spirit, God the. *See* Trinity.

Israel, originally the name given to Jacob (*Gn* 32:29), the grandson of Abraham, an ancestor of the Jewish people (ccc. 62-64, 839-840). *See also* Jews.

Jesus, a name that can mean 'God saves', is also called 'the Christ'. *See* Christ, and pages 20-33.

Jews, the name of the people drawn principally from the tribes who formed the ancient Kingdom of Judah, the remnant of the twelve tribes of ancient Israel (the Hebrews). The Old Testament is essentially the religious story of the Jewish people up to the time of Christ (*Compendium* 169, 276).

Laity is the collective name of all members of the Church who are not deacons, priests or bishops (ccc. 897-913; *Compendium* 177-178, 188-191).

Marriage in the life of grace refers to that sacrament (also called matrimony) by which a baptised man and a baptised woman are bound together by vows to an exclusive lifelong commitment to one another and to accepting and raising children. With this sacrament, God provides spiritual blessings for the fulfilment of these duties (ccc. 1601-1666; *Compendium* 377-350).

Mary, the mother of Jesus Christ and therefore also 'Mother of God'. Mary was given special gifts to enable her to fulfil her unique vocation. She was conceived immaculate (without Original Sin) and she conceived and gave birth to Jesus Christ as a virgin by the power of the Holy Spirit. Completely untouched by sin, she was assumed body and soul into heaven. Her many titles include being the 'second Eve' (ccc. 484-511; *Compendium* 196-199).

Messiah. *See* Christ.

Moses, one of the key figures of the Old Testament, led the people of Israel out of slavery in Egypt to a new land promised by God, and gave them God's revealed law as the pattern of a good and holy life (ccc. 62, 2056-2062; *Compendium* 8, 38, 114, 537).

New Testament. *See* Bible.

Old Testament. *See* Bible.

Original sin is the sin of rebellion of the first parents of the human race, the effects of which, including disordered desires and the loss of God's grace, have been passed down to all subsequent generations. The state of original sin is remitted by the grace of baptism (ccc. 396-412; *Compendium* 73-78).

Pentecost is a Jewish festival on the day of which, fifty days after the resurrection of Jesus Christ, the Holy Spirit descended upon his disciples in the form of tongues of fire, infusing them with spiritual gifts to proclaim the gospel. Pentecost is often referred to as 'the birthday of the Church' (ccc. 731-732; *Compendium* 144).

Peter was the leader of the twelve apostles chosen by Jesus Christ as the foundations of his Church on earth (*Mt* 16:18-19). Peter, the first bishop of Rome and hence Pope, died as a martyr on Vatican Hill during the reign of the Emperor Nero (c. AD 65) (ccc. 880-882; *Compendium* 109, 162, 187).

Pope is a special title of the Bishop of Rome. One of the distinguishing marks of a Catholic in communion with the Church is to acknowledge the authority of the Pope as the successor of St Peter, the leader of the apostles of Jesus Christ (ccc. 882; *Compendium* 182-185).

Prayer means speaking and listening to God, with a desire to be united to God and to do God's will (ccc. 2559-2565; *Compendium* 534-577).

Prophets are figures of the Old Testament, such as Elijah, Isaiah, Jeremiah and Ezekiel, who were chosen before the coming of Jesus Christ to proclaim God's message, especially exhortations to justice and holiness in expectation of a Messiah (ccc. 64, 218, 702; *Compendium* 8, 102, 140).

Redemption is the saving action of Christ on Calvary by which he ransoms us from sin and opens the door to everlasting life with God (ccc. 571-573, 599-623; *Compendium* 112-122).

Resurrection (of Christ). *See* pages 28-33 (ccc. 638-658; *Compendium* 126-131).

Sacraments are signs established by Christ that cause what they signify, healing us from sin and planting, nourishing or restoring the life of grace in us. The seven sacraments are Baptism, Confirmation, Eucharist, Confession, Anointing, Holy Orders and Matrimony (ccc. 1113-1134, 1210-1212; *Compendium* 224-232, 250).

Saint, a person who has become holy through grace, and especially those who enjoy the beatific vision of God in heaven, some of whom are officially recognised by the Church and given the title 'Saint' (ccc. 946-962; *Compendium* 194-195).

Salvation is the process, enabled by Jesus Christ and his Church, by which a person becomes a child of God by adoption, receives forgiveness for sins, and perseveres in the love of God to the end of earthly life. Salvation is final and eternal when a person enters the kingdom of heaven (ccc. 606-618, 1023-1029; *Compendium* 119, 230, 261, 366).

Satan (the devil). *See* Angels.

Scriptures. *See* Bible.

Sin is a deliberate evil action, which can be a thought, word, deed or omission. The special evil of sin is that it damages (if 'venial') or causes the loss of the life of grace (if 'mortal'), without which a person cannot enjoy second-person relatedness to God, culminating in friendship. Restoration of grace is usually by means of the Sacrament of Confession (ccc. 1846-1876; *Compendium* 391-400).

Son, God the. *See* Trinity.

Soul is the form of the body, and the soul of a human being possesses the special human capacities to know, to choose, and to love. Revelation teaches that a human soul, once created by God, is immortal and bears the imprint of personal identity beyond death (ccc. 362-368; *Compendium* 69-70).

Spiritual, in the broadest sense, means any kind or mode of being that is without matter ('immaterial'). The term is commonly associated with God or specifically the Holy Spirit, and a life of grace is often described as spiritual. Fallen angels (demons) are also spirits, however, so not everything that is 'spiritual' in a broad sense is automatically good (ccc. 367-368).

Supernatural, refers specifically in the Catholic faith to that which pertains to the life of grace, the Christian participation in God's life that is above or beyond nature (ccc. 1998-1999; *Compendium* 362, 384, 389, 420, 423).

Temple, the place of the true worship of God in the Old Testament period. The first Temple was built in Jerusalem by Solomon (c. tenth century BC) and destroyed in 587 BC. The second Temple was dedicated in 516 BC, after the Jewish exile to Babylon, and reconstructed by King Herod shortly before the birth of Jesus Christ, before being destroyed by the Romans in AD 70. The worship of the ancient Jewish Temple, where the Passover Lamb was sacrificed, prefigures the Eucharistic sacrifice today (*Compendium* 113-115, 538). *See also* Eucharist.

Trinity is the being of the one God revealed by Jesus Christ as three divine persons, the Father, the Son, and the Holy Spirit, in an unchanging and eternal communion of love (ccc. 232-267; *Compendium* 44-52).

Word (of God), as a title of Jesus Christ, expresses his complete divinity as the eternal Son of the Father and hence the perfection with which he communicates the being and message of God to us (ccc. 65-67, 101-104; *Compendium* 9).

What to do after the WHY? course

The WHY? course introduces the Catholic Faith. To learn more, it is recommended to read one or more of the four Gospels from the Bible, to examine the teachings and traditions of the Church, and to see how Catholics explain them. One systematic way of looking at the key teachings is to work through the articles of the Creed and the Ten Commandments, together with the commentaries on these matters in the *Catechism of the Catholic Church*. For each statement of the faith in the Creed, and for each of the Ten Commandments, try to think through some of the implications for daily life. Make a list of teachings about faith or morality that seem difficult to you and find out how the Church and Catholic teachers explain them. Make use of the *Catechism of the Catholic Church* and do not be afraid to ask difficult questions.

For those who are not already members of the Church, begin to pray regularly using prayers like the *Our Father* (page 33) and *Hail Mary* (page 47), asking God for the gift of faith. If you want to start the process of becoming Catholic, find a local Catholic church and start attending Mass, perhaps with a Catholic friend who can explain what is happening and what to do, but do not go to Communion until you have been baptised, received or reconciled. Contact the priest or parish office and inform them of your interest. You will probably be invited to talk to a priest or deacon who will ask you why you wish to enter the Church and talk through the steps towards a final discernment.

If you continue on in the process, you will probably start taking Catholic education classes, often in the context of the RCIA (Rite of Christian Initiation for Adults). During these classes, you should learn some of the history of the Church, the beliefs and moral teachings of the Church, and the proper order of celebration of Mass and other sacraments, such as Confession. Finally, if you are ready and willing, you will be baptised or received into full communion with the Catholic Church.